The Power Of A Pivot

How changing your mindset can bring you more joy in every aspect of your life

Written By:
Kim Howie
and
Nancy Werteen

Wishing you more joy every day! Kim ♥

Printed in the United States

Published by Gignere Publishing.com

Paperback: ISBN 978-0-692-95692-2

We dedicate this book to Heather Rodale, our
incredible Advising Partner.
Thank you for believing in us and our mission.
Your guidance and support gave our
"project" wings to fly!

FOREWORD

By Anne Alexander, former Senior VP/Editorial Director of Prevention Magazine
Author of two New York Times bestsellers, The Sugar Smart Diet and Win the Fat War
Founder of SoulCandy.com

Everyone needs a pivot-whether to change your mood, mindset or even-your life! And, thanks to Nancy Werteen and Kim Howie, the way to do that starts right here. In The Power of a Pivot, Nancy and Kim provide a gentle and gracious invitation to join them on life's journey to joy. Like a pair of girlfriend guides, Nancy and Kim open their hearts and candidly tell their stories to guide us through the thorns of regret, fear, perfectionism, and crisis to the wide vistas of love, success, legacy and ultimately to finding your authentic self.

As anyone in mid-life can certainly attest, it's easier to look on the bright side when your life feels full of sunshine and things are going your way. But finding the bright side – even the tiniest sliver of light – when you're in one of those inevitable, dark shady patches is a whole lot more work. And yet, that is exactly when we need to do it. That is when we need, as Nancy says, to "stop hard" and pivot.

What's so surprising is how much power each of us really has. By actively choosing where you are placing your attention and the choices you are making -- for the next five minutes or the next five years – sets the stage for what unfolds.

When you feel like curling up in a ball, calling it quits, or having a good long moan, you might want to envision Kim or Nancy tuning into your negativity soundtrack. I suspect they'd gently (and with good humor) nudge you to reconsider. "Is there perhaps an alternative interpretation?" I can almost hear Kim asking. Or Nancy might probe, "Is this really how you want to spend your precious time on the planet?"

Because, as they and their inspiring band of Women Coalition contributors make so clear in these twenty-four chapters, what you think about does become your reality. So, look up and look ahead. And, wherever you decide to focus your gaze, do so with the intention to find joy, and you will.

The Power of a Pivot:

How Changing Your Mindset Can Bring You Joy In Every Aspect of Your Life

Written By: Kim Howie and Nancy Werteen

Chapters:

1. The Wisdom Symbol
2. Love of Self
3. Mistakes
4. Crisis
5. Forgiveness
6. Success
7. Fear
8. Wisdom
9. Change
10. Perfectionism
11. Regret
12. Love
13. Trust/Betrayal
14. Passion and Purpose
15. Your Legacy
16. Refuel/Health
17. Self-Care
18. Friendship
19. What Would You Tell Your Younger Self?
20. What I Know For Sure
21. Vulnerability
22. Aging Gracefully
23. Finding Your Authentic Self
24. Joy: The Top 10 Ways To Connect To Your Inner Joy

Introduction

How many times in the last few days has someone asked you, "How are you?" If you're like me, you probably answered something like, "Fine. How are you?" Or, "I'm good. Busy. You?" Pleasant enough, but it becomes sort of a meaningless exchange, doesn't it?

Let me ask it again. ***How are you?*** But this time, stop and think about it. Really think about it. Are you happy? Are you content with your choices? Are you in relationships that are satisfying? Are you living in the present moment? Are you looking to the future with excitement?

If you aren't finding joy each day, if you're going through day after day without really intending to be happy, ***what you need is a pivot!*** You need to stop hard and make a quick change in the direction of your life. Why? Because life is a terminal condition. The clock is ticking for you, for me, for all of us. Don't waste a day of whatever time you have left.

Our philosophy at the Wisdom Coalition is that WE control our thoughts and actions and can shape the outlook and the day that WE want despite whatever is going on around us, and whoever is getting under our skin. Once you figure out how to do this, you'll be hooked. I know I am. When I first met Kim Howie, some days she would say, "I'm so joyful, I can hardly stand myself." Let me tell you, to be honest, I wasn't exactly sure what to make of that. Once we began the Wisdom Coalition however, and I learned how to approach life differently, one day I had an amazing realization. I woke up and began my day, which essentially means I have to let the dog out. Usually, I would approach this with some grumbling and mumbling about the cold and how long all the sniffing takes. This day, I stood outside enjoying the cool breeze, thinking it's okay if I'm cold, it will feel wonderful to warm up again in the house. I looked at the early morning sky and the setting moon and thought how beautiful it was. I glanced at the sniffing dog and thought, she's been a wonderful pet and loves us all so much. And wow! I realized I was completely filled with joy! It didn't matter that my daughter would soon be awake and blaming me for a lost sock or a paper that wasn't signed, that my husband would have the TV on too loud, that I had a to-do list for the day that reached the crook of my elbow. The joy was there, tangible and solid. I could hardly stand myself.

We believe in order to open yourself up to finding the joy all around you, you have to be able to evaluate who you are. You have to be able to take out and examine what we call "the mushroom topics," those subjects that grow when you keep them in the dark. We believe the key to a joy-focused life is being right with yourself. It is then that you can find, feel and fuel your own joy. But first, you have to figure out what's in your way. You have to uncover the roadblocks of excuses, grudges and criticisms and get rid of them. It is only through this self-examination that you can discover where the leaks are and repair them as quickly as possible.

In this book, we'll talk, laugh, explore and give you tools to make this shift in your life. We urge you to take a look at your endless to-do list of things that need to be picked up, put away and taken care of and put YOU on there. It seems we are all so busy we sometimes don't take the time to check in with ourselves, to make sure we're where we want to be and heading in a direction that will not only satisfy but thrill us. Why shouldn't we? Life is going to speed by anyway, and once it does, it's gone. There's no going back and doing it differently the next time.

THIS is the only time you have. So don't wait. Join us on a journey of self-discovery that will allow you to fuel your own joy and inner passion. And who doesn't want that?

We have structured this book with two predominant voices but also include wise words from many compelling and diverse women. Each chapter looks at a different issue so you can read from start to finish or just cherry-pick the order you'd like to read each chapter based on what interests you.

The two main voices you'll hear are the co-founders of The Wisdom Coalition, an idea that started because we saw how powerful joy and positive thinking could be and we felt a need to spread that concept to as many people as we could.

"We" consists of me, Nancy Werteen, television news reporter with WFMZ-TV69 in Allentown, Pennsylvania and Kim Howie, health coach, author, and designer of The Pure Energy Program. Kim is basically the expert here. She's well along her journey of self-discovery and makes it her life's work to counsel others on taking care of their bodies and minds. I'm sort of a knucklehead in the area of enlightenment who happened to be lucky enough to sit next to Kim one day as our daughters took a tennis class together. But I'm learning. Wherever you are on your journey to enlightenment, if you align yourself more with Kim or with me or somewhere in the middle, we're speaking here to everyone in hopes we can all learn something.

We have put together each chapter beginning with a quote from a woman in our Wisdom Coalition collaborative community from our past television shows or podcasts. Next you'll see my reflections acting as a springboard for each subject. Being a journalist, I've spent more than 30 years observing people and writing about them. Kim picks up the discussion next with her unique perspective along with techniques and tools from experts to help you take any challenge and turn it into a gift. We end each chapter with thought-provoking, self-reflection questions-the same things we asked ourselves before we started writing.

These voices will help you to examine yourself with honest words and soul searching discussions. We feel the Wisdom Coalition and our Well of Wisdom (http://www.thewisdomcoalition.com) are vehicles to provide each other with support and wisdom. Let us give YOU this gift. Come along with us on a journey that has changed our lives so that we can help you get the most out of yours.

Chapter 1-The Wisdom Symbol

Shonda Moralis
Psychotherapist, Mom, author of
Breathe Mama Breathe: 5 Minute Mindfulness for Busy Moms

"When we can pause, come back, and see a little more clearly what's in front of us — what we're thinking, what we're feeling — we're able to choose where to place our attention as well as our response."

Nancy Werteen:

At age five, my younger daughter began to be afraid of the dark. For months at bedtime, she didn't want me to leave her room and she'd say, "Leave a light on" and I'd say, "Now what's the difference? Your bedroom is still your bedroom, it's just that the lights are off." She'd give me that confused look that reminded me that reasoning isn't always the best tactic with little kids. So I did what I always do when faced with a quandary. I read something. I read a book on kids and bedtime fears. I latched on to a simple suggestion and she and I did it together.

We took small slips of paper. On one set, she wrote things that made her happy, brought her joy. On the other set, she wrote what made her feel afraid about the dark, about bedtime, about separating from me. We took the first set of papers, the "happy ones" she called them, and tucked them neatly under her pillow. And the second part she really loved. We took each of the papers "of the scary things" and one by one, she crumpled them up and threw them across the room.

"Really?" she said, "You won't get mad if I throw them on the floor?"
"Not this time," I answered.

Three nights in a row we did this and by the fourth night, she didn't ask for the light to stay on anymore. It was that easy. She simply needed to focus on the thoughts that she wanted and actively get rid of the ones she didn't.

And as often happens with kids, I learned from her. I found myself trying the same thing. I didn't do the physical exercise of throwing papers around because I frankly didn't feel like picking them up, but I let myself realize what thoughts were in my mind and how I could shift them to serve me better.

Sometimes you don't even realize what's buzzing around your head until you stop long enough to listen. And when you listen…really listen… you can challenge those thoughts and figure out which ones are working for you and which ones are working against you. And then YOU get to decide what stays and what goes instead of the other way around, instead of your thoughts controlling you.

For me, looking around inside my head is not my first choice of activities. To be honest, I'd rather do pretty much anything else, but I've learned cobwebs hide everywhere and need to be cleared out once in a while. And having a more defined sense of who I am has helped me to stay the course, stay true to the person I want to be.

When I think back at my younger years, I remember being very confused, especially if there was a nice-looking guy involved. I had an idea of my true self, but I didn't pay enough attention to it, and I let people and circumstances swing the pendulum inside of me that was my center.

This summer, I watched my college-aged daughter navigate her first serious relationship. One evening we were all eating dinner together and she proceeded to go on a litany of explanations about the best bathrooms at school for certain bodily functions. I wondered how she could talk about that with her "gentleman caller" sitting at the table. And then it hit me. She's herself! She isn't changing who she is to suit a guy. Now believe me there's a lot more to her than talking about bathroom habits but I love that she doesn't change for anyone. She's sure of herself and confident in who she is. I know I wasn't that put together at 19. I have to admit, I spent a lot of years floundering.

When we began to develop the idea for The Wisdom Coalition, it was Kim who came up with the Wisdom Symbol and what it represents. Unlike me, Kim is a master at managing feelings and talking about them. And as with most things about The Wisdom Coalition, I think I remember that she sent me a text at 5:00am when she couldn't sleep because she had this life changing idea. When she told me, the light bulb went on in both of our heads.

Figuring out who you are and staying true to that is the solid path to inner peace and joy. At the end of the day, you need to feel good about who you are, the decisions you've made and the things you stand for. I get it now. Took a while. Read on to hear from Kim who always explains it better than I do!

Kim Howie:

I attended a conference several years ago where a number of experts spoke on topics related to health and wellness. Most speakers talked about the benefits of good nutrition and healthy lifestyle practices such as exercise and stress reduction. This was wonderful information that reinforced what I already knew and had been sharing with my clients on a regular basis. But there was one speaker in particular who stood out and spoke on a topic that truly transformed my life. She spoke about the connection between joy and health. Up until that point, I had never considered that joy played a role in my health.

She began by asking a question "what, besides your family, your friends and your job, brings you joy?" This question threw me into a tailspin. I had never once given this a thought! I was just going about my life living from day to day, trying to keep all of my balls up in the air without allowing any to drop, never stopping to think about what brought me joy. She then asked us to turn to the person next to us and share our joyful activities. I struggled to find an activity that sparked joy. I was feeling pressured, and even considered making something up (like I love to knit, even though I wouldn't even know how to hold a set of knitting needles). It was then that I realized that I was not alone! So many of us were "getting through life" rather than living a joy-filled life!

She then went on to explain how our bodies respond to our thoughts (both positive and negative) by producing chemicals in the form of hormones and neurotransmitters (brain chemicals) that have profound effects on our overall health and wellbeing. She shared study results that clearly showed the connection between joy and our ability to maintain or regain our health. This lecture was truly life changing for me both professionally and personally!

Professionally, as a Health Coach, my mission is to help people be proactive with their health. I take my clients on a journey that I refer to as building awareness. I help them make the connection between what they eat and how they feel. Then we work together to add in more of the foods that nourish their bodies while crowding out the foods that aren't serving them. I spend a lot of time talking to clients about eating real whole foods and making healthy lifestyle choices, but joy was never part of my wellness plan. Now, after attending that conference, I tell clients that mindset is the foundation for healthy living. And I know this for sure based on my own joy journey!

Personally, I made the decision that very day that I was going to prioritize joy in my life. I was going to remove all things from my life didn't bring me joy. It was a revolutionary idea for me, that just like with foods, I could build awareness around things (people and activities) in my life that did not serve me. And just like junk foods, I could crowd out the things in life that were stealing my energy by adding in things that brought me more joy.

I remember coming home from the conference and telling my husband that I was no longer going to spend time with people or doing activities that didn't bring me joy. I was bracing myself for his reaction, but he simply said "ok, sounds good to me!" Although secretly I'm sure he was wondering if he would be doing his own laundry from now on.

This sparked an incredible adventure for me. I began sifting and sorting through life with my new barometer "does this bring me joy?" I was feeling good about the progress I was making and how I was taking control of my health and wellbeing by focusing on joy.

Then one day, a few years later, I had an incredible aha moment ~ I realized that ***I was the one who determined the amount of joy I received from the people and activities in my life***! And although this may sound trivial and elementary, it was truly transformational for me;

I realized that **"I CONTROL MY OWN THOUGHTS!"** And that those
thoughts are the foundation for joy. Up to that moment, I was living
life backwards and allowing my thoughts to control me. I was allowing
outside circumstances and other people's actions to steal my joy. I was
operating in a reactive fashion. I'd allow traffic to stress me out and I'd
allow other people's actions to make me angry, all along placing the
blame on those outside circumstances and allowing them to dictate my
level of joy.

I was giving my power away to other people and circumstances
that were outside of my control. The simple realization that I have little
control over what others think, do or say, but I have 100% control over
how I choose to respond or react with my thoughts, actions and feelings
was truly life changing and empowering!

I started to pay attention to what things I allowed to steal my joy
in life, and I slowly began shifting my thinking around them. I love
the quote from Dr. Wayne Dyer that says, "when you change the way
you look at things, the things you look at change!" I started to shift
my perspective on life and was amazed at how much more joy I was
experiencing.

I recognized that I could train myself to find joy in everything in life,
even doing laundry! I began looking for positive aspects and practicing
discernment. Joy became my daily intention. I started a joy journal
where I write down all of the things and people in my life for which I am
grateful. This was the first step in building what I now refer to as my joy
muscle. It's not always easy to maintain, but just like any other muscle, it
requires constant flexing and training to keep it growing.

I've found that one of the keys to successfully maintaining my joy
muscle is surrounding myself with positive people. Having a community
that shares my passion for finding joy in the journey of life was the

impetus behind The Wisdom Coalition.

As Nancy mentioned, the Wisdom Symbol is at the center of what we believe to be true at The Wisdom Coalition. The purpose of the symbol is to remind us to live our lives from the inside out (with our passion and joy driving our thoughts, actions and feelings) rather than from the outside in (allowing circumstances and the outside world to influence our thoughts, actions and feelings). And to always remember that WE control our thoughts and actions! The truth is that when we increase the quality of our thoughts, we instantly elevate our feelings and are open to experience more joy and unlimited bliss in our lives.

The Wisdom Symbol exemplifies the mind, body, spirit connection to our inner light. It is a visual representation of the relationship between our thoughts, our actions and our emotions, and their ultimate effect on our core energy.

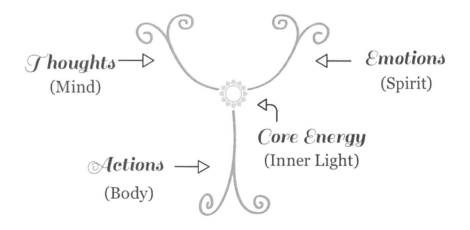

The Wisdom Symbol

The spirals represent:
expansion, connection and balance

Thoughts ⟶ (Mind)

⟵ Emotions (Spirit)

Actions ⟶ (Body)

Core Energy (Inner Light)

Here is a detailed explanation of the design and meaning of the Wisdom Symbol itself.

The symbol is comprised of 3 Y's coming together to create one larger Y (which represents our ultimate purpose.) Each Y represents a different dimension; thoughts, actions and emotions. The sunflower in the center represents our core energy (our heart, our inner light, and our truth.) The bottom Y represents the body; with our actions rooted, grounded and balanced by our core energy. The upper Y's represent the mind and spirit, like open arms reaching towards the sky, welcoming a life filled with joy. The spirals at the ends of each Y represent expansion, connection, and balance.

Each Y is growing out of the heart-center, representing the fact that our core energy (inner light, passion, purpose, truth or whatever word resonates with you) is the foundation of our Y. And therefore, when we are connected to our Y, our core energy drives our thoughts, actions, and feelings enabling us to live a joy-filled, purpose-driven life.

At The Wisdom Coalition, we believe by sharing our wisdom with others, we stay connected to our passion and purpose, allowing our inner light to shine for all to see, and igniting the light of those around us. In doing so, we are essentially spreading the joy of life!

The Wisdom Symbol serves to help us stay connected to our ultimate goal at The Wisdom Coalition, which is to live life with purpose-centered thoughts, actions, and feelings enabling us to uplift others we encounter on our journey through life.

Chapter 2 - Love of Self

Annarose Ingarra-Milch
Author of Lunch With Lucille
Motivational speaker, entrepreneur

> *"When I think of those three words, "love of self" I think of strength. When I hear strength, I think of power. When I hear power, I think of self-empowerment. And self-empowerment is what directs me and propels me. Simply put, 'love of self' is always the foundation."*

Nancy Werteen:

Let me tell you, menopause has not been my friend. Back when I was pushing 50, I thought this whole menopause idea sounded pretty good. No more periods. Where do I sign up? But now that I am on the other side of it, there is so much more to it than that. The first thing is what my husband and I affectionately call, "deflate-gate." Basically my boobs were there one day and gone the next. And when I looked for them, I couldn't find them at first but then discovered they had both slipped down and were now happily snuggled inside my abdomen. Hence the major purchases to Spanx® and other Spanx-like organizations. My poor husband has watched the progress of my body through our credit card bills. In my 30s, there were the Victoria's Secret® purchases. The 40s, time for Soma® to lift this and squeeze that and now Spanx® . Sigh.

Okay, so I said the boob issue was the first thing, but you know what? I'm not even going to get into the second, third, fourth and fifth thing because we'll be here all day. But despite these changes and the comments I really can't stand about how I look pretty good "for my age," something I wouldn't expect has happened. All my adult female life, I bellyached about my body. This wasn't big enough and that wasn't small enough. And I surrounded myself with good-natured buddies who did the same. And while I joke about my changing form, I really don't care that much anymore. I guess part of that has to do with age. Listen I'm not ready to go out shopping with a mu-mu on and no bra, although no one would probably notice the bra thing, but I think I am finally understanding that loving myself has nothing to do with how I look.

I remember when my older daughter turned 15 or so and one day we were walking on the beach and I had this awful realization that the guys on the beach weren't checking ME out, they were looking at HER!!! As horrifying as that was on so many levels, there was something liberating about passing the baton to the younger generation. I suddenly realized "at my age" I am kind of off the hook. No one expects me to look that great anymore so I don't really have to worry about it.

And don't we do that as women? Define ourselves by how we look! I'm ashamed to say I am guilty as charged. When I think about all the years I wasted thinking I wasn't good enough. Before writing this, I rifled through some old photo albums and found a picture of myself at 19. Wow. How did I even eat food with a belly that flat? But even then, I felt down on myself. It's crazy to think about that now.

As an adult woman, I've realized that my looks don't define me. Instead, when I look back at my life, I know I've been a good mom. I know I make my husband happy, deflate-gate and all. I know my parents love me. They say I've been a wonderful daughter. My sister says she's so happy she can lean on me. These are the things that define me. I'm lucky enough to have a few real friends who I can call at any time, who listen to the worst parts of me and don't turn away.

My only wish is that I had this epiphany sooner. I work hard now to help my daughters understand how much they have to offer the world that has nothing to do with flat bellies and tight butts. Thankfully, I picked a father for them who never doubts what they can do and who they can become. He's their biggest cheerleader and never sees limits and you know what? They don't either!

And by the way, so now you know my secret. I'm the granny of the Wisdom Coalition. Not really a granny, but I could be one. It is what it is. For some reason I had the audacity to have a baby at 40. But how lucky am I that the plumbing worked and she's here and she's wonderful. I may be the oldest one at the bus stop, by a long shot, but that's okay. Who I am is not the definition of a number. Would I love to have my 23-year-old body back? Of course, but I really kind of love this age in spite of the physical challenges. I've never felt more empowered and confident in my whole life. What sense does that make? I should have felt more confident when I was younger but I grew into it I guess.

My husband and I actually have the same birthday and on this last one I was a little reluctant to let the number cross my lips. He said, "When you're 65, you'll be wishing you were this age and had the body you have today!" I hate it when he's right. But that's a good point, isn't it? I realize now I should savor the moment. Make the most of every year. I should focus on and be thankful for the things I have and forget about the things I don't.

I'm not perfect. I never was and I never will be. But I can try my best. I can be the best friend that I can, the best mom, the best daughter and the best wife. This is who I am. And that's pretty good if you ask me.

Kim Howie:

I often say that I've lived many different lives in this one awesome lifetime. One of those lives started when I got married for the first time at age 19 to a man ten years my senior, who also happened to be an alcoholic and a nasty drunk. I truly believe that we are on this earth to live, learn and grow from our experiences; and that was a wonderful lesson in the making! I learned so much about myself and found my inner strength with my ability to walk away from a potentially life-threatening relationship. But to this day I am grateful for the awareness I gained about the importance of self-love.

Fast forward 28 years, and I now know that love of self is the key to healthy and happy relationships. When I am not taking proper care of myself, whether it's eating foods that don't serve me or deviating from my wellness plan in other ways, I find that I don't feel good physically or emotionally. And oftentimes that results in my projecting those feelings onto others and behaving in ways that perpetuate those feelings to continue inside me. This quickly becomes a cycle of self-defeating thoughts, actions and feelings. It's with awareness that I am reminded that I am in control of how I choose to think, act and feel. I remind myself that with awareness I create healthy habits. This is always the first step to making a much needed YOU-turn in my life. I use the term YOU-turn in my practice to encourage clients to turn their focus around and put themselves back on their priority list.

I believe that self-care is rooted in self-love. And when we make healthy choices in life, such as eating foods that nourish us and honoring our body by getting ample exercise and rest, we are demonstrating to ourselves and others that we love and appreciate ourselves. And the inverse is true as well, when we choose not to care for ourselves, we are sending a message to our mind, body and spirit, as well as those around us, that we don't love ourselves and that, therefore, we are not worthy of love; and ultimately, it's okay not to treat us with love.

For a long time, my sense of self was dependent on what others thought and said about me. I worked very hard to please everyone in order to feel loved and appreciated. I've learned over the years that striving to please everyone is a futile effort that typically results in frustration, resentment and great unhappiness on my part. In the end, what matters most is that I live my truth and I allow others to do the same.

Through my studies in positive psychology, I was introduced to a series of assessments that helped me identify my strengths, talents and values. The results of these assessments astonished me, as I was surprised to see that qualities that I had always thought of as personal weaknesses were portrayed as strengths. This was the beginning of a wonderful journey towards self-love and self-compassion. One of these strengths was sensitivity. I recognized that I had been beating myself up for many years for being a sensitive person, trying to eliminate this self-perceived weaknesses, yet in reality it was a strength of mine. One that in hindsight has helped me to cultivate authentic connections throughout my life. Flipping my thinking on several of my strengths has helped me to see myself and others through the lens of love.

I believe that the secret to unconditional love of self and others is to recognize that we are all doing the best we can with what we have and what we know. And as Maya Angelou said, "when you know better, do better." And although I sometimes need to remind myself, as this "earth school" is a lifelong learning journey, I do know in my heart that my capacity to love others and for others to love me is directly related to my capacity to love myself!

Thought-Provoking, Self-Reflection Questions:
1. What are your personal strengths?
2. What do you love most about yourself?
3. What qualities do you want to strengthen?

_____

_____

_____

_____

_____

_____

_____

_____

_____

_____

_____

_____

_____

_____

_____

_____

_____

_____

_____

_____

_____

_____

_____

_____

Chapter 3 - Mistakes

Debra Fraser-Howze
Sr VP of Government and External Affairs
Orasure Technologies

> *"Redemption is a religious concept but if you have faith in yourself*
> *and faith in the higher power which is caring for other people, you*
> *begin to understand that everybody makes mistakes and that there*
> *is redemption and that when you get to the other side of the*
> *mistake the only thing you have to do is learn from it."*

Nancy Werteen:

I really had to think long and hard about mistakes. Of course I've
made them. I've made a ton. Who hasn't? But it's more the definition of
"mistake" that has me perplexed. Some things or decisions are clearly
mistakes. The time I decided to have three martinis in a half hour after
being alcohol free for an entire pregnancy and a year of breast feeding-
big mistake. And then there was the time I decided to look in the rearview
mirror of my minivan to put on lipstick as I was pulling out of the garage.
The side view mirror and I soon found out THAT was a mistake. So there
are mistakes that are just things we know we shouldn't do.

Professionally, there's a list there too. Once during a live shot I said,
"bastard" instead of "pastor." Another time during a six hour election night
live show, I said "erection" instead of "election." Now obviously I didn't
mean to say those things. They were more accidents than mistakes
I think brought on probably by fatigue or distraction or who knows
what one is thinking to say erection instead of election. My copy has
had mistakes at times, of course, despite fact checking but that's not

deliberate either.

My first memory of a really big mistake is from high school. I was a senior and for some convoluted reason I can't quite remember, my friend came up with a grand plan that I would drive a gaggle of girls home in HER mother's car because she had something to do and then meet her at her house with the car. Sounds perfect. Well I drove everyone home and headed for her house. I can see myself so clearly in that Country Squire-remember those station wagons with the wood panels on the side? If you're over 45, you'll know what I am talking about. Anyway, it was May and I had the windows down and my arm out the window. Van Halen blared "Runnin' with the Devil" from the AM/FM radio. So cheesy now but to me back then, I was on the top of the world. At that time in my life, driving meant freedom and I couldn't get enough of it. Only problem was that my car was a VW bug, a small car. So driving a station wagon, it's easy to forget there's a bit more in the back end. As I raced around some windy roads we used to call "roller coaster roads," I'm sure I pushed that poor station wagon in ways my friend's mom never did. You know where this story is going. I screeched around a corner too tight and another car was coming in the opposite direction. I swerved and then overcorrected and slammed the back end of the car against a tree. Holy $#@t! What just happened? I wasn't sure so in my 17-year-old wisdom, I decided to just ignore it and the scratchy noise coming from the back end. Never even stopped the car. Okay, so that was all clearly a mistake proven by the consequences that followed.

I think as you age you figure out how to avoid mistakes. These days I know I can't have more than two glasses of wine for instance and I always wait to put on my lipstick until I'm fully out of the garage, but what about those other decisions that may or may not have been mistakes? There are people I loved and probably shouldn't have and people I probably should have loved but didn't. There are jobs I didn't take and jobs I did. And parenting, you talk about a mistake minefield. I remember one time when my older daughter was about 4 years old. She loved to get all suited up in her snowsuit and take her sled down a hill in our backyard. One day we went out after an ice storm and I never even thought to check the hill. Just put her on the sled and gave her a push. As she rocketed down the hill, I realized it was a sheet of ice and she was heading straight for a bank of trees. I raced behind her slipping and sliding and screaming, "ROLL OFF THE SLED!!!" because she was on course to hit the largest tree of all. I couldn't catch her. Somehow, she leaned or something and veered about an inch off course which took her out of harm's way. Stupid of me but was it really a mistake? Should I have known there would be ice there? Maybe, but it's not as clear as knowing you shouldn't speed in a car or get distracted while driving one!

So I think there are decisions we make that aren't the best but can't really be called mistakes. I felt not checking the hill for ice was a mistake at the time, but now I'm not so sure. As a first-time mom, I double-checked everything that kid did, touched or was exposed to. I didn't make a decision to do something irresponsible but it was dangerous just the same. Mistake? Maybe yes, maybe no.

What about relationships? There are men I've trusted I shouldn't have. Mistake? You could argue that but how is trusting in someone a mistake? How is loving someone or taking a chance a mistake? Taking a risk might be a mistake but not taking a chance on the honest character of another person. How else can we find true connections? And if it doesn't work out, it's not our mistake, or is it? People don't come with warranties. We love who we love sometimes with abandon, without wondering if we'll make a mistake or if we won't.

I've worried plenty about trying to avoid mistakes. When I had my first baby, I remember thinking I would drop her or slam her head into the door frame when I was walking from one room to another. We worry a lot about mistakes, don't we? Mistakes feel awful. I remember having a friend in middle school who always used to say, "If one of us falls in the cafeteria, we'll have to change schools." Ridiculous and hilarious now. But back then, we had another school as a backup plan which made no sense because we went to public school and didn't even realize we couldn't change schools if we wanted to. But why would the thought of a mistake bring us to such an extreme place?

I stepped on my glasses a couple months ago. Mistake? Of course. But now I have a little holder that I fashioned on my night stand to put my glasses in when I take them off to sleep. Ah-ha. So I learned from my mistake, didn't I? So maybe mistakes are just little lessons that we need to have so we can do something better, more efficiently, with more ease, more structure, more confidence. I think that's true. I think we can stop beating ourselves up about mistakes and look at them as steps on a ladder. We can't get to the top until we walk on each one. And maybe I've walked on more than someone else but that's okay too. My journey is mine, messy as it may be.

Kim Howie:

I have come to believe that everything in life is happening FOR me rather than TO me. This helps take me out of the victim mode, but it also forces me to look for the lesson or the silver lining in all of my life experiences. This simple shift in mindset has proven to be transformational in my life. I like to look back at past experiences and connect the dots to see how what felt like a mistake at the time later proved to be a pivotal moment that redirected my steps toward a better outcome.

Oftentimes when we are in the midst of what feels like a mistake, it's difficult to see the light at the end of the tunnel, and recognize that we are learning as we go through life. This journey is full of twists and turns, and although we think that we'd like to get from point A to point B in one straight easy-to-travel line, it's the ups and downs along the way that make life interesting. They provide contrast and perspective to help us realize all that we have to be grateful for.

I do believe that we make mistakes in life in order to grow and learn from them. So I try to see them as learning opportunities rather than mistakes. Fear of making a mistake oftentimes keeps us stuck and holds us back from moving forward in life. While attending a conference recently, the presenter stated that every time we make a mistake, rather than beating ourselves up, we should say "how fascinating!" and recognize that we just learned something new! I love this idea, and have been using it ever since to help me move forward when I feel frozen after making a mistake.

The key to learning from our mistakes lies in self-reflection and owning our part in the mistake (rather than blaming others), otherwise we will continue to make the same mistakes over and over again. I do believe that is the way the world works. If we don't learn from our mistakes, they will continue to show up disguised in different clothes, until we finally take responsibility for our actions and make different choices going forward in life.

I also believe that we create our own reality by the way we choose to perceive life's events. It always amazes me to see how two people can experience the same event, but both come away with completely different stories about what occurred. I see this play out in my marriage all the time. I'll say to my husband "you have your reality and I have mine!" How I process the event is very different because I run it through my personal filter that has been refined throughout my life based on my personal experiences. Yet he has his own filter, and so the event comes through looking very different to him. This realization has been extremely helpful for me in understanding that I need to choose happiness over the need to be right and offer compassion rather than dish up blame for any perceived mistakes on his part or mine.

I think that what one perceives as a mistake another can perceive as an opportunity for growth. A simple shift in perception can make all the difference!

Thought-Provoking, Self-Reflection Questions:
1. What is your definition of a mistake?
2. How can you choose to look at a specific mistake differently?
3. What mistakes in your life have helped you grow?

_____

_____

_____

_____

_____

_____

_____

_____

_____

_____

_____

_____

_____

_____

_____

_____

_____

_____

_____

_____

_____

_____

_____

_____

_____

_____

Chapter 4 - Crisis

Amy Edgar
Founder, Children's Integrated Center for Success
Mother of a special needs child

> *"I would say it's really important to understand that crisis has a beginning, a middle and end and a timeline; and sometimes when you're in the middle of crisis it's hard to see that."*

Nancy Werteen:

I never set my alarm clock. I don't have to. Every morning, my silly dog decides 5:30am is a great time to remind me how much she loves me. Her snoot is just about the height of my bed so she can easily just ram it in my face with a chorus of whining and an accompanying round of disgusting licks and well...I'm awake.

She's always been what I call a "mischief maker" and it always involves stealing food. What that dog didn't do when she was younger; from jumping on the stove and knocking over an entire pot of chicken soup to eating frozen Alaskan King Crab legs whole to stealing our food right off our plates more times than I can count! I tried everything to break her of the food stealing habit but there was always a payoff for her and so none of my tricks worked. I remember one time we walked in a St. Patrick's Day parade with my daughter's school so we wrapped a nice green bandana around the dog's neck and took her along the parade route. We matched the steps of the folks around us and every time there was a lull and we slowed to wait for this float or that child to pick up some candy, our Nikki would casually suck down the Doritos or cotton candy and even a whole hamburger of one of the unsuspecting spectators along the parade route.

But these days her knees are too bad to steal off my counters anymore. She will sit in the kitchen and stare at me with a look that remembers the good old days. Her light is going out. We're not sure how old she is. She was my older daughter's appendicitis gift when she was 8 years old. As she was being wheeled into surgery, in a desperate attempt to do anything to take away her pain and fear, I blurted out, "When it's all over, you can have a dog!"

So we went to the Humane Society several weeks later and brought Nikki home. She's at least 11 now, maybe 12 and a big dog-a Chesapeake Bay Retriever-who retrieves nothing and whose annoying snoot is now entirely gray. These days when she wakes me, I never feel like I should be mad at her. How many more days do we have together? There can't be many and I have this feeling I should savor every minute.

My parents take her sometimes on the weekends when we go away or just to get their dog fix and I am always shocked at how much I miss her. No one is as excited to see me when I come home and no one cleans the kitchen floor like she does. At first, I'm thrilled she's gone. I can open the front door with abandon. I can leave food out anywhere I like. But that lasts for about an hour. And then I think, "It's so quiet. I could use a little nuzzle right now." I think I see her when I don't. Something is missing.

She will be gone soon and it will be a crisis for us, for our family. I've been trying to prepare my daughter, the younger one. It will be so difficult for her. So we talk about it. We sit with Nikki and pet her, pour our love into her as much as we can. She's teaching us how to say good-bye in that amazing way that pets do.

Being in television news, you witness a crisis every time you go to work. The worst things you can imagine: a child goes missing, a house burns, a wife is murdered and found by the side of the road in a garbage bag. And you meet people going through hell. You talk to them and they tell you how they feel. It's an amazing gift. I've always felt the gravity of making sure I represent the people I interview with tact and grace and fairness. It's astounding how some people are able to rebound from a crisis in a way that seems impossible. Over the years, I remember plane crashes, car accidents, murders, fires and every now and again there's that person who calmly says something like, "We'll get through this. We're okay. We're blessed." Wow. Really? Some people seem to understand they just need to surrender to the ups and downs of life. What in the world can that remarkable resiliency be attributed to? For some, I think it's that they've taken enough hard knocks that they know how to get back up. For others, it's sheer determination. For some, it's faith.

I have a dear friend who when I call her with some crisis that isn't necessarily a real crisis, will always remind me of something we did from years before. She'll say, "Remember that? Time passes, doesn't it? And when it does, everything seems far away. This will be a distant memory too." She is right. Now that I think of it, she's one of those people who is a rock in times of crisis. I'm not saying there's anything wrong with falling apart. But I think we can learn from others who've been there and back about how to keep our heads from slipping under the water because that's so easy when we get pushed down.

And I don't think you need a major event to let something set you back. A crisis can be big or small don't you think? It can be something awful, but it can also be something that just upsets our day, our flow, our plans for what we wanted. The key seems to be to practice balancing the scales and really embracing the realization that nothing is perfect and nothing is guaranteed.

When I first started to become close enough with Kim that I felt free to complain about things from time to time hoping she'd join in my rantings about this or that, every time and I mean EVERY time, she would calmly redirect my focus. "Oh you were stuck in traffic? How wonderful, you had a chance to listen to something you like on the radio." Or "You had to deal with that difficult person? What a great opportunity for you to practice your patience." Hmmmm. Talk about shutting a person down. But you know what? After this happened a few times and she continued the conversation with that sunny attitude she has, I thought, she's onto something.

Frankly, it feels so much better to snap out of a negative mood with one sentence. It feels great to take an annoying situation and turn it upside down. Flips the focus, shifts the power in another direction. So I decided to try it, with Kim's help, of course. I'm still not that great at it but sometimes I get it right and when I do, it's fantastic. Makes me feel untouchable. And my life has literally changed. I'm not kidding. Now I listen to what I say and I try to pull in reckless words and put out productive ones instead. It's nice. It's peaceful. It's working. Listen to her and you can give it a try too.

Kim Howie:

I've heard it said, "when you feel as though you are falling out of an airplane, just hold on and it will be over soon." This is what comes to mind when I think about a crisis. It will pass; and I believe that I will be stronger for having gone through it.

I've come to see crisis as a relative term. What some perceive as a crisis is an everyday occurrence in other's lives. I remember a while back coming home to the realization that we had no running water in our house. This seemed like a crisis at the time, as I needed to shower and make dinner, both of which required running water. Then I suddenly realized that there are people in other areas of the world who never have running water. They need to walk for miles to collect water every day of their lives just to survive. This helped to put my "crisis" into perspective.

When I feel as though I'm in the midst of a crisis, I like to imagine rising up and looking down at things going on in my life from 10,000 feet above and realizing just how small my "problems" are in the grand scheme of the world. Although I don't typically advocate for comparison or spending too much time looking in the rearview mirror, sometimes it does help to put life events into perspective. Looking back, I can see that this too shall pass.

I've recently learned a wonderful tool for managing stress that comes in handy during a crisis. When I feel my stress level rising, I stop and assign a number to the stress. I ask myself, "on a scale from 1-10, how stressful is this situation in the grand scheme of your life?" This exercise is twofold, as first it forces me to stop and take a step back from the current situation, essentially interrupting the cycle of stress-inducing thoughts that are perpetuating the stress, and second, it forces me to become mindful of the specifics that may be artificially exasperating the physical and/or emotional stress, essentially putting it into perspective.

I believe that if we can learn to manage stress in our lives, we can handle crises more effectively. And, of course, this has an important impact on our overall health and wellbeing. So my professional advice to my clients is to be proactive about stress management. Create a daily routine that includes stress reduction practices such as meditation or scheduled breaks throughout the day for deep breathing and mindful movement. Like anything else in life, this takes time to feel natural, but eventually you will realize that it's become a habit. And ultimately it will help you to remain calmer, not only in the face of a crisis, but throughout each and every day of your life.

Thought-Provoking, Self-Reflection Questions:
1. How do you handle crisis?
2. What can you do now to help you navigate crisis more effectively going forward?
3. What have you learned from a specific crisis in your life?

_____

_____

_____

_____

_____

_____

_____

_____

_____

_____

_____

_____

_____

_____

_____

_____

_____

_____

_____

_____

_____

_____

Chapter 5 - Forgiveness

Liz Jordon
Survivor of childhood sexual trauma and trauma sensitive yoga instructor
Clear Path Wellness, Emmaus PA

> *"When people have the idea that, 'Doesn't that (forgiveness) get someone off the hook?' It's not about that. It's about you. It's about taking care of you and get there in your own time, in your own way. Build your team of people who will help you."*

Nancy Werteen:

One of the first times my younger daughter ever threw up, after destroying a section of the family room carpet with her sudden explosion, she turned to me and said, "Mommy, I'm so sorry I spilled." Poor cutie. Now in those days of sippy cups and sticky fingers, spilling on the cream-colored family room carpet usually meant a big deal. Even in her discomfort, her first thought went to thinking she should be forgiven. Of course, I responded as any mom would, that is was okay and she didn't mean it. This whole exchange confused her. "Is it okay to spill juice if it is in my mouth first?" "Is it okay to spill if I didn't mean it?" "What about ketchup?" We worked on this litany of questions for weeks.

I remembered all that as my mind churned thinking about the subject of forgiveness. Oddly enough, as I mull over these chapters, I find myself waking up at 3:00 or 4:00am with a million thoughts in my head. So here's my mental vomit on forgiveness that came to me this morning. It's the list. There's this list in my head of all the people and who did what when. She did this back in 1997 and he did that in 2008. I really didn't realize that list was there. I thought about forgiveness and suddenly this list of grievances appeared. Do you have a list too? How many times have you pulled that list out and rattled off the details of some offense perpetrated by someone in your life now or then? I really thought I had nothing to say about forgiveness. I am good, I thought. Now, I'm not so sure. So I pulled the list out and went through it, detail by detail, and thought carefully about what I am holding on to and how to let it go. Really, let's be done with it.

I think for most of us, the first people we have to forgive are our parents. Can you remember back when you thought your parents knew everything, were perfect and had superpowers? Most kids think this way and one day it becomes evident that we might have been wrong. We realize our parents are just flawed human beings and in a sense we have to forgive them for that-for not living up to the unrealistic expectations we set for them. And then we have to forgive ourselves for thinking up such an impossible goal in the first place.

We learn to forgive I think from a very young age and develop the skill as we get older and more and more people give us reason to have to forgive. The situations become more complex certainly but there are even small things we have to forgive every day, aren't there? Yesterday it was the person who cut us off in traffic, the cashier who was snide, the child who was unkind to our own child. Today, the list continues.

As a reporter, I've seen incredible acts of forgiveness. You may remember when ten Amish school children were shot inside their one room school house back in 2006. As horrific as that act was, the family members of the children reached out to the shooter's family within days offering forgiveness. Astounding. But what an amazing gesture and gift for that family-to stop beating themselves up for a split second in the grace of this offering.

And there's the real issue-there's a gift in forgiveness-not just for the person who did the offense, but also, for us. Those Amish family members moved on with their lives absent of the enormous burden of hate, resentment and anger. They still had terrible grief of course, but at least they could lighten their load just a bit.

When I look at my list and really consider everything on there, I'm thinking, what's the point of hanging on to it? There's no award given out for the most bullet points. There's nothing I get from mulling it over. Now, I'm making it sound easy but I know it's not. We recently taped a Wisdom Coalition television program with two women who were sexually abused by their father. Our focus was how they were able to forgive him. They both spoke of a long journey, of the immensity of the issue, but also of a freedom that came from letting it go.

It's complicated for sure. But I think realizing what you might be holding on to is the first step to a freer spirit. I think the list is part of the baggage we carry around every day. I've read my list for the last time and I am going to do my best not to add anything to it going forward.

Kim Howie:

Forgiveness is a gift you give to yourself! Marinating in anger or resentment keeps you stuck in the past and prohibits you from engaging in and enjoying the present moment. It can feel as though you are trapped in a maze, with no way to escape.

When I'm feeling trapped in the maze, I remind myself of the fact that anger doesn't serve me in any way. This simple awareness helps to bring me back to the present moment and allows me to put the situation into perspective. For example, if someone cuts me off on the road, and I feel myself getting angry, I'll ask myself, "What good does it do to get upset? How is this serving me?" This prompts me to remember that my anger at them doesn't hurt them in anyway, but it does hurt me!

Holding on to pain and anger has a detrimental effect on our health. Just notice how your body feels when you think about someone or something that made you angry or upset. Your muscles tighten, your heart rate increases, cortisol begins to flood your bloodstream causing inflammation that leads to a whole host of diseases including heart disease, Alzheimer's Disease and many forms of cancer.

Oftentimes we are holding on to anger toward others for pain they may not even know they have caused us. I've heard it said that 90% of our relationships take place inside our own heads. At first I thought that was absurd, but once I pondered it for a while I realized that it may even be higher than that!

We often create stories in our head as to what others are thinking or feeling. These stories may or may not be valid. It's important that we pay attention to our thoughts and build awareness around how often we make assumptions about what others are thinking or the meaning behind the words they are speaking. Once we recognize that we have created a story, we need to challenge our thoughts and ask ourselves, "is there a chance that I may be wrong?" The only way to test the validity of our story is to open up and ask the other person. I've come to realize in my life, particularly in my marriage, that this step is huge and oftentimes opens the door for deeper authentic connections.

My innate tendency is to sweep things under the rug, as I don't like conflict; but I've learned over the years that those things build up and then surface at inopportune times. So I've learned to address things as they happen, and try to do so in a kind and loving fashion.

What I've found in my marriage is that there are usually three sides to every argument; my story, my husband's story, and then the truth lies somewhere in the middle. Of course we both feel as though our story is right, but that's because we are experiencing it through our own filter of reality.

In addition to the stories we make up in our heads, we sometimes unknowingly project our feelings onto others. We might be feeling uncomfortable in a situation and project that feeling onto others, walking away thinking that they were not nice or welcoming to us. Meanwhile they may be thinking that we were not friendly or open to their presence. Again, this is about perception, and I try to remind myself of the fact that we tend to see things, not as they are, but rather as we are; meaning that we are seeing everything in life through our own perspective.

For me, forgiveness is often a two-way street. Many times I find that I am so focused on my own hurt that I fail to recognize the role I may have played in creating the issue or the pain that I may have caused the other person. This is where open dialogue and an open mind help to shift my perceptions.

When it comes to forgiving loved ones, I like to use a visual technique to imagine projecting my love towards them. While seeing that love embody them, I begin to focus on all of their wonderful qualities and remind myself of why I love them (rather than focusing on what they said or did that hurt me). This simple tool oftentimes helps me to escape the maze!

Perspective taking is another helpful tool. Shifting our perspective involves changing the lens through which we look at the person and/ or the experience. Attempt to put yourself in their shoes and see things from their perspective. In order to forgive, we need to look through the lens of compassion and try to understand that the other person is a human being who is likely struggling with their own personal issues. This idea of shared humanity has been transformational for me. Recognizing that we are all more alike than different, and we are all working on our own issues in our own unique way.

None of us is perfect, and we all have light and dark within us. I've heard it said that oftentimes when we are broken, that's when the darkness seeps out, but it's also those cracks that allow the light to get in.

The final, and sometimes the hardest step in forgiveness is letting go. A friend gave me the book, *The Life Changing Magic of Tidying Up.* It was a wonderful read with great advice, but what I loved most was the idea of using joy as a form of measure to determine which items to hold on to and which to let go. I've found this concept to be just as useful in cleaning up my mind as it is in cleaning up my home. For me this means sifting and sorting through my thoughts and memories to determine which ones bring me joy and which ones I need to let go of.

Once those less than joyful memories have served their purpose, it's time to say "thank you for helping me to grow and expand, now I am choosing to let you go." To me this is what forgiveness is all about, finding the gift or the lesson in the experience, and then letting go of the pain.

Thought-Provoking, Self-Reflection Questions:
1. Is there someone in your life that you need to forgive?
2. How can you see them or the experience through the lens of compassion?
3. What is holding you back from forgiveness?

_____

_____

_____

_____

_____

_____

_____

_____

_____

_____

_____

_____

_____

_____

_____

_____

_____

_____

_____

_____

_____

_____

_____

_____

_____

Chapter 6 - Success

Anne Baum
Vice President Lehigh Valley for Capital BlueCross

"To me success is your ability to pursue your passion and balance
the things that are important to you so that you can spend
your time where that time is most well spent for you."

Nancy Werteen:

In college, I used to say to myself, "When I can buy red shoes, I will know I made it." That was the litmus test for success for me at that time. See I worked my way through college, you could do it in those days. I jammed all my classes into three or four days and worked pretty much non-stop the rest of the time. I went to a commuter college so we all worked and lived in run-down apartments and tried to figure out how to pay the rent and the utilities, eat and put gas in our cars. As difficult as those years were, they were also a huge incentive to make sure I graduated on time and moved to a job that paid what we used to call a decent wage.

The college I went to had campuses on Long Island and in Manhattan so once a week or so, I would take the train into the city for classes. Invariably, because this was New York City and the 80s, I would pass a store window display that held a dazzling pair of red shoes. Red. Then I would see a woman sauntering down the street with shiny red shoes on her feet and I was smitten. Now to get out of Manhattan and back to Long Island, I would have to go to Penn Station right near Madison Square Garden to get on the train. This is right in the heart of one of the city's major shopping districts. Macy's Herald Square is close by, all 11 floors. I think the second floor is still almost all shoes. So I would torture myself time and time again and visit the red shoes, sometimes even daring enough to try them on. Once I looked at the price tag, I had to put them back. I just didn't have the money.

So for years I held that mantra in my head but by the time I could actually afford red shoes, they really weren't in style any more. You know I bought a pair anyway? But it soon became clear that I would only visit them in my closet now instead of that shiny window display. I never could find an outfit to go with them. They went off to a second hand store one day but they were my badge of honor. They proved to me that I had succeeded.

I have noticed as years go by, my standard for success has changed and morphed with life's surprises and circumstances. At one time it was getting pregnant and after 28 hours of labor, it was getting that baby out! At another time it was managing a broken vertebra in my back, two kids and a stomach flu. There were times success has been dealing with a difficult relationship, being brave enough to walk into a room full of people when I knew no one, or figuring out my daughter's math homework.

Success has so many definitions. In the worst of times, success has been breathing in and out, getting through the next minute, trying not to fall apart. In the best of times, it's been watching my beautiful 19-year-old daughter become a person I could only have dreamed of her being. It's been finding an incredible new friend at a time in my life when I never expected it. It's turning to my husband of 25 years and knowing we're both imperfect but we love each other and have built a solid marriage, home and family.

Being successful and being able to pay for the red shoes is one thing but being the kind of person someone wants to hang out with-even if you have no shoes at all-is really the meaning of success, I think. I heard someone say that success is the becoming of a person. I love that phrase. Success is someone who tries, tries to be the best she can at all things in the best and the worst of times. And if she reaches a goal, fine, but for me I didn't even want the red shoes once I had them. The journey to get there really marks the success; that I was brave, that I tried and that I have loved and am loved.

And we're all successful in our own ways, don't you think? Whatever success means to you, I'm sure you're trying your best to get there. And once you do, I'll set aside some red shoes for you!

Kim Howie:

When I was younger, I thought success was all about getting a job with a big title and making lots of money. I remember the day that I was promoted to Assistant Vice President and I thought I had finally become successful. Yet suddenly that old definition of success was no longer enough; I needed to become Vice President in order to be truly successful. I feel that kind of success is a never-ending quest for more and better. It's never enough, therefore, I'm never enough!

My new definition is that success involves joy and having a sense of fulfillment and meaning in life. I believe the true purpose of life is growth and expansion, but most of all it's about fulfillment. I look for opportunities to evolve and continually remind myself that life just keeps getting better and better! To me this is success!

I've come to recognize that the joy is in the journey, not in reaching the ever changing, and therefore elusive destination. Having goals is great, but it's important to recognize that whether or not you achieve them doesn't define you or your worth. Achieving all of your goals doesn't necessarily make you successful, especially if you've achieved those goals at the expense of others or the expense of yourself.

We live in a world that can be cutthroat and extremely competitive. Although competition can be good if it propels you to strive to do or be your best, it can also be detrimental if it results in behaviors that are not in alignment with your values. We intentionally created the mission of The Wisdom Coalition to include the words "collaborative community" because we recognize that there is a lot of unhealthy competition amongst women these days. We sometimes put others down in order to help us feel better about ourselves or more successful as women. We've created competition where it doesn't need to be. Rather, we can spend our time and energy lifting each other up and in turn helping one another recognize that we are all "enough!"   We should be celebrating each other's successes along the journey of life!

Thought-Provoking, Self-Reflection Questions:
1. What is your definition of success?
2. How has that definition changed over time?
3. What would you tell your younger self about success?

_____

_____

_____

_____

_____

_____

_____

_____

_____

_____

_____

_____

_____

_____

_____

_____

_____

_____

_____

_____

_____

_____

_____

_____

_____

_____

_____

Chapter 7 - Fear

Carmen Twillie Ambar
President of Oberlin College, attorney, mother of triplets

> *"The way to deal with fear is to light that flame of desire because when you desire something, you can boost that flame. And you do that by talking to people who are really supportive, you go and get yourself prepared for the new endeavor, you can boost that flame of desire and desire always trumps fear."*

Nancy Werteen:

When Kim and I first came up with the idea for The Wisdom Coalition, we made a pact to tell no one but our husbands. We carried on this way for a few months. We rationalized it by saying we weren't ready, didn't have all the details worked out. But we were afraid of a million things like failure, as I recall. And that fear kept us in this weird limbo that prevented us from really doing much of anything to bring our idea to life. After a while, we realized we would have to tell other people. Ridiculous to imagine we wouldn't. We kept our safe secret guarded between the two of us but eventually came to a point when we decided we would let the proverbial cat out of the bag. And you know what? We kind of stumbled all over the place at first. We had so many reservations and questions about what people would say and how we would answer. There was really a paralysis of sorts that we basically created on our own by focusing on all of the things we were afraid of.

Naturally, we began to work out the jitters and the kinks and once we pushed through our reservations and started talking, no one has been able to shut us up since! I realize now that once we got the confidence in ourselves and our idea, our fear went away. And this takes me to my point. I think self-confidence has a lot to do with fear and not just professionally. If you believe in yourself, you aren't afraid to stand up for what you want in all of the relationships in your life. If you believe in yourself, you aren't really afraid of too many things actually because you think you'll do okay in any environment you're put in.

One of the most common things I hear as a television reporter is, "I could never do what you do, I'd be too afraid to go on TV!" I smile and nod and don't tell them how I used to have to wear a maxi pad when I first did live shots because I was so scared I thought I'd literally crap my pants! We're afraid of what we don't know how to do usually. I'm afraid of crafts and math. They make me sweat and feel a little queasy. For me now, TV is easy. But give me a canvas and a paintbrush and I am ready to run screaming from the room.

Fear is normal and healthy but it crosses a line when it holds you back. You have to recognize it for what it is and push through the uncomfortable feeling it gives you. Fear is like that really loud close talker with the pickle breath who pins you into a corner at a party. You want to get away but you get stuck and find yourself watching the mouth move and not even hearing the words anymore. You zone out. You stay on the sidelines of life. You miss opportunities.

I say spit in fear's face every chance you get. Whatever you're afraid of, if you try and succeed, it will feel better than you know. And if you don't succeed, so what? You tried. And that's an accomplishment of its own.

I think fear is a huge issue for women. I always notice when I interview women for stories, they're always more afraid than the men. Their hair's not right. They don't want to say the "wrong thing." The men don't care. Okay, some do. But most men are happy to put themselves out there, whatever the question I am asking. They're pretty confident what they're saying is good and intelligent. And they never worry about their hair.

Ladies, I say look fear in the face and give it a hard shove out of your way. Move forward with confidence and leave fear behind. And if you can't do it alone, reach out to a friend and have her help you. There's no sense being afraid, unless you're walking in traffic. Fine. But I, for one, am so sick of fear and being fearful in my life. I hate the idea that fear has power that I have given it by being complacent and not having enough confidence in myself.

Recently, I was working with a woman on her on-air presentation. We worked out a scenario and I asked her to do a run-through. She started talking but continually shifted her gaze toward me, searching my face for approval. As she talked, I could see her getting more and more nervous. I stopped her and pulled her aside. "Why do you think you're here?" I asked. She looked at me sort of confused. "Because I have a lot to learn?" She responded, her voice rising at the end of her sentence like she was asking a question. Now, let me tell you this is a brilliant, talented woman but the thought of being under a microscope clearly terrified her. I said, "No, you're here because your boss believes in you, because I believe in you, so why don't you believe in yourself?" Again, she hesitated. This time she looked down and when she looked back up, I noticed some tears and figured I'd hit a sore spot. "I don't know," she said. I said, "Listen, don't wait for me or your boss or anyone else to validate you. You know you can do this. You know the material. Don't wait for anyone else to tell you that you can do it. Believe in yourself first." Don't we do this as women? We wait to see what others think? We wait to decide what to wear to the party until we ask what everyone else is wearing. Let's be done waiting.

When I look back at all the ways fear has stifled me, it really makes me mad. For Kim and I, we were scared, but every small success drove that fear farther and farther behind us. We don't even feel it anymore. Well, maybe a little. But now we recognize it for what it is and we talk each other through it. We are each other's cheerleaders. And there's no way fear can compete with that!!

Kim Howie:

Fear is like a poison that gets into your system and slowly shuts down your ability to function. It literally sucks the joy right out of you. The irony is that it's oftentimes a poison that we inject into ourselves. Fear usually starts out small and then snowballs into a giant avalanche. I can remember several years ago I was asked to give a talk to a group of people about the topics covered in my first book, *The Simple Recipe For A Healthy, Balanced Life*. At first I was really excited about the opportunity to share my philosophy with others, but then all of a sudden out of nowhere I began to worry that I might forget the words once I stood up in front of everyone. In hindsight, this seems so strange, as they were MY words, how could I forget them? It's not as though I was going to be reciting facts and figures that were foreign to me. But the more I focused on the fear, the worse it became. I remember standing in my office and trying to practice my speech hours before the talk, and when I opened my mouth, I couldn't get the words to come out! The fear had literally paralyzed me. I somehow made it through the talk, but vowed to never speak in public again!

Fast forward several years and I find myself back in the position of speaking in public. I needed to let go of the past and not allow the fear to hold me back from sharing my message. However this time it's a new challenge; it's television! Now I need to remember my words AND worry about how I look while delivering them! I recognize that this is a different type of fear. This fear is about putting myself out there and truly being seen (not just heard). I'm opening myself up to criticism from an audience that I fear will be critical. This is not just ordinary fear, this is downright terrifying to me! And on top of that, I am worried that I will let my amazing business partner down in the process.

Worry and anxiety are just cousins of fear. But the antidote to fear is action. I knew the only way to move beyond the fear was to not allow it to keep me stuck. I had to feel the fear and do it anyway. I remember hearing once that self esteem is pretty stable throughout life, but self confidence needs to be built through action. Once we take the first step forward, each step that follows will get easier and easier until we eventually feel confident and leave the fear behind.

It's important to know that we ALL feel fear at times in our lives. It's nothing to be ashamed of or diminished by. Simply knowing that we're not alone, and that others have experienced these same feelings may be a comfort when fear begins to build. Recognize that you can disarm fear by moving forward and building confidence with action.

Don't allow fear to hold you back and steal your joy. And, as Nancy mentioned, reach out and ask for help. Fear is one of those mushroom topics, it grows when we keep it in the dark! Let others shine the light on it and help you move through it. I know I could not have taken on the role of co-hosting a television show without Nancy shining the light and leading me out of the darkness of my inner fear!

Thought-Provoking, Self-Reflection Questions:

1. What fears are you battling now?
2. How are your fears holding you back in life?
3. Who can you ask to help you tackle your fears?

_____

_____

_____

_____

_____

_____

_____

_____

_____

_____

_____

_____

_____

_____

_____

_____

_____

_____

_____

_____

_____

_____

_____

_____

Chapter 8 - Wisdom

Heather Rodale
VP Community Outreach Rodale Inc.,
Founder of Healing Through the Arts, cancer survivor

"Sometimes wisdom doesn't just come from smart, educated people, it comes from people who know how to live and to survive."

Nancy Werteen:

Whenever my dad left for work, my mom would stop whatever she was doing, wipe her hands on the dish towel and walk over to him with the same phrase: "Have a safe tour." A New York City firefighter in one of the busiest houses in Manhattan, she knew when he left, he might never come back. He worked in Rescue 1, an elite squad trained to do just what the name implies, rescue. So in the midst of any fire, helicopter crash, building collapse or other catastrophe in midtown Manhattan, his unit went in first to rescue anyone who needed help. Imagine that. You drive up to a burning building and you're the first one raising your hand to go in.

It became a delicate dance they did around the danger they both knew existed. And when those phone calls came-that he fell through a roof, put his hand through a window, was trapped in an elevator of a burning high rise-we waited for the next call to tell us if he survived and how badly he was injured. She knew what was at stake when he went to work, but she also knew she couldn't convey those feelings to us kids. This is a wise woman.

My mother grew up in Germany during World War II. She was

11 when the war ended and still to this day can barely talk about it. When she does, it's with carefully measured words and an emotion that seems like the eye of a storm. After the war, her family lived in an occupied Germany behind the Iron Curtain. She literally escaped before the physical Berlin Wall was built, fleeing to a refugee camp in West Germany with others desperate for freedom from a government and way of life that held few choices and little opportunities. She earned a nursing degree and while in West Berlin, noticed a young man from the United States in his military uniform who was stationed in the city. They married and she found another completely new life in Brooklyn, New York. My mom is a person with life experiences very different from mine.

Every month when I was a kid, I'd watch her making a package for her mom and dad and brothers and sisters. She'd put in things like coffee, cigarettes and toilet paper, the necessities we had that they didn't. "Why can't they buy their own coffee?" I'd ask. I didn't understand about Communism or shortages. We lived in the Long Island Land of Plenty after all. But once she became a US citizen, she was free to travel back to East Germany with a few stipulations from each government. During most Christmas seasons, we would go to her tiny hometown for three weeks with its cobblestone streets and coal stoves that left a strange smell in the air and a gritty cloak on just about everything. It was an exhausting and confusing trip that took us days and through quite a few very tense checkpoints. I didn't understand everything, but I knew enough to know I should keep my mouth shut. She had this brown suede coat she would wear because in those days, you dressed to travel. I used to sit quietly behind her while the Russian soldiers rifled questions at her in a language I didn't understand. I would write my name in the fabric on the back of her coat, trying to keep calm and quiet like she said, my fingers tracing the letters over and over again.

I grew up knowing my family was different. I can still see my cousins gathering around us to gape at our clothing and possessions. Everything in their world was controlled, even what they watched on TV, so we looked, acted and sounded like nothing they had ever seen. Somehow, with this dynamic, we played in the backyard and threw a ball in the street and laughed and found some common ground.

But I've always known my mom had a wisdom that comes from hard times. She has a way of summing things up as most moms do. "Every pot has a cover" she used to say when I was lamenting about finding the "right guy." "I don't care if he's green, blue or purple, as long as he's good to you," she'd say. We always talked about everything. When something goes wrong or something goes right in my life, she's the first one I call. And wisdom? Yeah, she's got that.

I think Heather is right, that wisdom comes from people who have struggled and endured. They understand what it takes to survive. They know how to put things in perspective. I have made a living out of listening to people and latching on to the wisdom they have to share. It's the best part about being a broadcast storyteller. Everyone has a story and something they've learned that can teach us all. We just need to listen.

Kim Howie:

When Nancy and I began talking about our idea of creating a safe place for women to share wisdom, we had a vision of a collaborative community, but no idea what we would call it. We tossed around names for several days, but none of them fit just right. I spent countless hours searching on Thesaurus.com to try to find words that summarized the feeling we were trying to convey with our mission. Then one day my daughter, who was ten years old at the time, said something so incredibly wise to me. She said, "you know Mom, you are thinking too much; it will come to you as soon as you stop trying to think about it." How did she get so wise at her tender age? It was at that moment that I realized that we ALL have wisdom, regardless of our age or stage in life. Although some wisdom comes from lessons learned through life experience, some is simply innate.

Over the years, I have learned so many lessons from watching and listening to my children. Sometimes it's like looking into a mirror and seeing myself in their actions, and other times it's as though they invoke a response from me that is intended to teach me something about myself or life in general. I remember looking forward to teaching my children all of the lessons I've learned to help them on their journey in life. But ironically, I've found that I have learned as much (if not more) from them about life than they've learned from me. I watch them navigate life with ease, simply following their hearts' desires and thriving on pure joy. Yes, I've learned so much about the meaning of life by watching my children!

I believe that we are surrounded by opportunities to learn each and every day; but we need to remain open to the lessons at hand. This involves the important skill of listening. Listening to others as well as tuning in and listening to our own inner guidance.

Oftentimes we get stuck in one way of thinking and close off the channel to acquire wisdom. My personal mantra is "I'm open and flexible." To me this means that I am willing to listen and learn, am not attached to the outcome, and am open to change. Sometimes I need to remind myself of that fact, but for the most part I try to live my life in accordance with my mantra.

Thought-Provoking, Self-Reflection Questions:
1. What does wisdom mean to you?
2. Who do you turn to for wisdom?
3. What wisdom do you have to share with others?

_____

_____

_____

_____

_____

_____

_____

_____

_____

_____

_____

_____

_____

_____

_____

_____

_____

_____

_____

_____

_____

_____

_____

_____

Chapter 9 - Change

Tina McGovern
Women empowerment and success coach

"Change is challenging because we get ourselves into what I like to call
our 'mental fence' state. You have a fence up at your house to keep your
children in the yard or other people out and so, you're in your own little
bubble. When it comes to change, it's the same concept. We get stuck
with complacency. We get stuck with where we are but once we do
(break out of that fence) it's beautiful on the other side."

Nancy Werteen:

My favorite movie of all time is Planet of the Apes-the original with

Charlton Heston-how can you not love it? I remember being in college

and my housemates and I would sit around on a Sunday afternoon

and recite the lines along with the movie. We'd pick who would get to

be Cornelius, Zira, Taylor and of course Nova didn't have any lines so

she was the easy one. Our small living room become our own personal

Rocky Horror Picture Show. If we weren't too hung over, we'd pull some

props out for the reenactment. There was no internet then, no computers

even; it seemed like a fabulous way to spend an afternoon at the time.

Anyway, I love this movie because I'm a sci-fi junkie but more than

that, the premise has always fascinated me. Not that we will be taken

over by apes but that the idea we have of our lives and who we are can

change and be upended in an instant. Think about it. A birth, a betrayal,

a death, a diagnosis, a move, a new job, and suddenly everything is

not what you thought it was. And sometimes, our sense of who we are

changes too. As things around us change, we wonder if we really are who we think we are. This grappling is what I gather is our search for our sense of self. As a person "of a certain age," there have been times in my life that I've struggled to keep my footing on my own personal sense of self cliff. If the things around me weren't what I thought they were, then who the heck am I? I've had to look long and hard at times to find me.

It all changes. Everything changes, every day. When my kids were little and going through some difficult phase, like needing to eat every meal from the same plate or insisting on wearing a Cinderella Princess costume for a year-and-a-half, you think it's never going to change. When is it ever going to get better? And then one day it does. The difficult time changes and suddenly seems so far away. Now that little girl in the Princess costume is in her second year of college and looking back at photographs of her, I can't even imagine what she was like back then.

The other day I had to tell my little daughter that our neighbors are moving. "What??!!" she shrieked. Now let me tell you about these neighbors. We have keys to each other's houses. When our dogs were young, we would get them together every day for an hour or two so they didn't eat our houses. And the kids! Well, first we had to walk them across the street and play kickball with them. Then we would let them get together and watch from one of our houses. And now, the boys across the street are out most days and my daughter will yell, "Can I play across the street?" and out the door she'll go. The neighbors are part of our lives, from driveway conversations, to Halloween parties and Christmas cookies.

I tried to explain to her that we'll still see them and sometimes things change. At that, she shouted, "Why do things HAVE to change?" Good question honey. She would love for things to stay the same, but change is all around us. Every day. Every time we make a move, open our mouths, have a meal. We don't think about it in that way of course but it's always there. Some changes are expected and you can plan for them, while others come in like a bull in a china shop.

Some years back, after a ridiculous incident when my girls were pretending to be Sumo wrestlers and the older one was flipping the younger one, sitting on the ground I heard myself say, "Go easy girls" right before the little one's kneecap or heel or something slammed into my back. In the hospital when the nurse came in and said, "You fractured your L-2", my husband and I both smiled and nodded. She walked out and I said, "What's an L-2?" He answered, "I thought you knew!" Once we called the nurse back in and understood the severity of my injury and listened to the instructions: "no movement of the torso for 12 weeks, back brace with steel rods, might require surgery," we knew change had slammed us in the face once again.

I spent the first few days crying and having a huge pity party. My sweet husband moved a recliner into the family room because I said there was no way I was going to be holed up in the bedroom. We set up a landing station for me. He moved the television and put a desk within reach. I cried some more. I didn't want to watch television and it still hurt to try to reach the desk. He took my socks on and off, made me food, took care of the girls. I cried again. I wanted to put my own socks on and take care of the girls myself. By day four, after I cried some more, he and his always positive attitude gave me a good talking to that I sorely needed. I began to realize that the more I fought this situation, the worse it would be. Yes, it was a huge change and I wanted to hate every minute of other people taking care of me and not being able to do things for my kids. But I began to see that if I stopped looking at things the way they USED to be and started to look at this new normal, I could make adjustments and still have some control over my life. I discovered online grocery shopping, found a wonderful group of ladies from a local church who would come in once a day to check on me and throw a load of laundry in, and my then 14-year-old daughter started to learn how to cook.

After some time, I actually began to enjoy myself. I read a ton of books, took a nap every day and made some wonderful connections with friends and neighbors who brought us food, drove the girls places and even plunged our toilet once or twice. Their generosity and our thankfulness for it elevated those relationships to a wonderful new level. What's more, once I gave in and stopped fighting the changes, the adjustment and the new life was so much better than I expected.

It's so difficult to adjust to change but it seems that the more we focus on our inside and not what's going on outside, the better we'll be. Once I realized I was still who I was, everything felt better. I think that's a clarity that comes with age. For me, that's what the Wisdom Symbol is all about. No matter what is happening around me, what's going on inside will remain familiar. I may change too but I won't lose who I am, what I believe in and what I hope for. So, go ahead world, make your changes. I got this one.

Kim Howie:

Change may feel challenging when we are in the midst of it, but oftentimes it's leading us in a new direction that will prove to be for our benefit. I like to think about change as an opportunity for growth. The key is being open to accepting the unknown and allowing life to unfold as you travel this amazing journey with all of its twists and turns.

When I look back at my life, I can clearly see how all of the pieces came together to create this amazing puzzle! One that continues to unfold each and every day. Appreciating change is about embracing life and recognizing that the contrast of challenging times helps us to strengthen our joy muscle and prepares us for the future.

We all experience highs and lows in life. It's easy to be joyful during the high times, but the challenge is to remain joyful even in the low times and find the gift in each new day. This is the foundation of unconditional joy (finding joy regardless of the current conditions in your life')

Every day I set the intention to stay present in the moment and find joy in life by focusing my attention on positive aspects. Some days this is easy while other days it is more challenging. For that reason, I have been working for several years now to build awareness around triggers that keep me stuck in a pattern of negativity. Oftentimes this happens when I am focused on the past or longing for the future.

I find that awareness is the first step to embracing change. In this process of building awareness, I became aware of something that I hadn't realized I did quite often. I noticed myself thinking (and even saying) "I just need to **get through** _____ (you can fill in the blank with the holidays, this day, or some event that was challenging for me). I realized that I was not enjoying life, but rather just "getting through it."

Once I became aware of this joy-limiting behavior, I started to work on replacing those negative thoughts and feelings with ones of excitement around the action that I was identifying as challenging. This involved changing the lens and looking at those challenges as opportunities for growth and expansion, ways to learn a new set of skills and strengthen my joy muscle.

Change is inevitable; and like it or not, things are going to change. Why add the stress of resisting change when it's going to happen anyway? I believe that our fear of change is rooted in the fear of the unknown. However, we can choose to look at the unknown differently, and rather than focusing on the fear, we can think of it as a surprise or an adventure. Imagine how boring life would be if we knew what was going to happen every moment of every day. It would be like reading a mystery novel for the second time, where you already know the ending.

I love this quote by Oprah: "Embracing and welcoming change is the essence of living a dynamic life." Embracing change is a goal in progress for me, one that I continue to strive towards and hope to someday master!

Thought-Provoking, Self-Reflection Questions:
1. What do you fear about change?
2. What changes have proven to be positive in your life?
3. How can you embrace change going forward?

_____

_____

_____

_____

_____

_____

_____

_____

_____

_____

_____

_____

_____

_____

_____

_____

_____

_____

_____

_____

_____

_____

_____

_____

Chapter 10 - Perfectionism

Jennifer Perreault
Counselor, veteran, postpartum depression survivor, mother of 3 boys

"Perfectionism doesn't exist. We put these stigmas on ourselves or we allow society to put these stigmas on us and it is never going to be attainable. Your perfection is who you are and what you strive to be."

Nancy Werteen:

Growing up, if we were having company, my mom brought out the rake. We had one of those shag carpets that were so popular in the 70s. They were like a huge compilation of pieces of yarn standing straight in the air but as soon as you walked on the carpet, the fibers fell down and showed every footprint. So, with company coming, my mom would literally rake her way out of the room so every fiber stood straight up toward the ceiling in all their shag glory. And then, of course, no one was allowed to walk on the carpet until the doorbell rang.

It was around this time that my foray into perfection, or perhaps I should say imperfection, began to percolate with my hair. After all, it was 1976 when Farrah Fawcett graced us all with that iconic image of her and her fantastic hair. Every day of ninth grade, I used every curling iron, twist curls and hot rollers I could get my hands on to try to create that famous Farrah Fawcett flip in the front of my hair. Some days I came pretty close, but it only took about five minutes of being out in the rain or the wind and my stick straight hair pretty much flopped back into its normal position.

In my household, we tried for perfection but soon realized we were far from it. With three teenagers in the house, my dad used to go to the junkyard and buy all different parts of Volkswagen Beetles. He had a huge shed where he stored all these cars and their car parts. When one of us needed a car, he and my brother, like Dr. Frankenstein and his sidekick, would somehow piece together a car that somehow, sort of, functioned. But let me tell you, these cars were far from perfect. Sure there were cosmetic issues; however, the real beauty was that they lacked things like heat, windshield wipers, or the ability to start when you turned the key. The one I had the longest only started maybe once every tenth time you tried. So wherever I went, I had to park on a hill. Why you ask? Well, a stick shift car can start if you do something called "popping the clutch" which essentially means you have to get the car rolling, then you have to jump in, put the clutch all the way to the floor and then take your foot off the clutch quickly as the car is moving. The car will lurch forward and usually start, if you're going fast enough. All my girlfriends knew if I was driving, we were all pushing the car until it started.

Anyway, my mom would get the most functional cars first but when they developed too many problems, they were handed down to one of us. She had this mostly black Beetle that worked through each of us. It literally had rust spots so severe, you could see the road going along the edges of the floor on the passenger side. This was okay and even made for some good conversation, until it rained. My dad's big solution was to keep a quilt and a stick in the back seat. If you were unlucky enough to be in the passenger seat in the rain, to avoid a tidal wave in your face if the car went through a puddle, one was instructed to hold the quilt down with the stick. You can't make this stuff up.

So one day, one of the cool girls at school asked me for a ride home. Now she rocked the Farrah Fawcett flip and even had 12 pairs of corduroys in every color. I was so honored and excited to be taking her home. This was my ticket into the cool kids' club for sure. We laughed and chatted as we walked toward my mostly black car and I was on top of the world until I realized it was cloudy and, gulp, looked like rain. There was no way out of this now. We got in and I sheepishly explained the quilt and the stick. She looked at me and raised her eyebrow in the air. Maybe the rain would hold off. No, as soon as I started the car, the skies opened up. It was pouring. "Really…you need to hold the stick on the quilt," I told her, "Like really hold it with all your might." She gently put the stick on the quilt and I desperately tried to avoid every puddle and then it happened. Right through one I went. The quilt shook under the crest of a wave that blasted onto the undercarriage of the car. There was no stopping it. The tidal wave lifted the quilt and sprayed water right in her face, Farrah Fawcett flip and all. Needless to say, I didn't make it into the cool kids' club after that fiasco.

I've never been good with perfection. By 13 years old, I was 6 feet tall with hands that reached all the way down to my knee caps. My sister and I were so tall, my mom used to make our clothes. Lovely gesture but my mom hated sewing. We'd pick out some pattern all excited and I can still see her with fabric all over the kitchen table and every German curse word on the planet flying out of her mouth. Her efforts produced sleeves that were long enough yes, but they weren't exactly a seamstress's dream. Sorry mom. Now that I think of it, this was the same routine she went through trying to bake a cheesecake. She was always on a quest for the perfect cheesecake that didn't deflate after it came out of the oven. She'd pull it out and we'd all gather around and hold our breaths. "This is the one!" She'd exclaim-although with her German accent it sounded more like, "Dis is de one!" Just when it seemed like she finally got it right, the silly cake would flatten in the pan and that string of German curse words would go flying once again.

But you know what? My mom always thought I was perfect. She still does. I would come down to the kitchen and say, "How does this outfit look?" She'd say, "Perfect." "How's my hair?" "Perfect!" I would always argue with her. "I'm sure it's not perfect. You're just saying that." But that didn't stop her. She'd say "No, it's perfect!" with just as much enthusiasm. To her, it was unthinkable that I could be less than perfect. I grew up knowing we weren't perfect but also knowing that to her, it didn't matter. I try to do the same with my girls.

I've realized that perfection is impossible. I can't think of one time in my life when I have attained it. When I first started in television, they all said my Brooklyn accent would be my undoing. I spoke too softly. I wasn't cut out for the business. When I got pregnant, I skipped the chapters in *What to Expect When You're Expecting* about long labors, large babies, morning sickness and hernias. I wasn't doing any of those things. My pregnancy would be perfect. Right. Vomited every day for 16 weeks, got two hernias, spent 28 hours in labor giving birth to a nearly 10-pounder. Far from perfect.

I say to my kids, "Just do your best" every chance I get and I tell them I'm not perfect at anything. I just do my best and hope that's good enough. It's all you can do. And these days, my car has a solid floor, heat, windshield wipers and even air conditioning. That's pretty perfect I'd say.

Kim Howie:

You may have been conditioned to think of perfectionism as a strength, something that drives you to try harder and do better in life. However, experts say that perfectionism is not correlated with drive for success. They explain that drive for success is intrinsically motivated, and therefore, not dependent on the approval of others; while perfectionism is externally motivated and ultimately rooted in our fear of what others will think of us. And furthermore, perfectionism often gets in the way of success, as we can get caught in the loop of not yet good enough, and find it difficult to move forward. Hence the saying, "don't let perfect be the enemy of done."

Dr. Brene Brown, in her book *Daring Greatly*, says that we are living in a culture of scarcity. Meaning that we oftentimes feel as though we are not enough (good enough, smart enough, successful enough, thin enough, pretty enough, etc.) This culture of scarcity drives our need to be perfect, and the feeling of never good enough creates incredible stress for many of us both emotionally and physically.

Dr. Brown says, "what makes this constant assessing and comparing so self-defeating is that we are often comparing our lives, our marriages, our families, and our communities to unattainable, media-driven visions of perfection, or we're holding up our reality against our own fictional account of how great someone else has it."

It's important to recognize that perfectionism is simply a perception; our perception of others, as well as our perception of ourselves. When we compare ourselves to others who we view as perfect, we tend to look at them and assume that they have it all together. From the outside their lives may look perfect, but on the inside they may be struggling with feelings of not being enough as well. Dr. Brown goes on to say "Nostalgia is also a dangerous form of comparison. Think about how often we compare ourselves and our lives to a memory that nostalgia has so completely edited that it never really existed: "Remember when.....? Those were the days...."

When it comes to our self-perception, we are often our own worst critics! We say things to ourselves that we would never think to say to another person. Our expectations are inflated, and then we get caught up in the "stinking thinking," telling ourselves that we are not good enough, and/or that others are perfect. But the good news is that WE control our thoughts, and therefore we can shift our perceptions. I like to refer to this action as changing the lens. In doing so, we are choosing to look at things differently. My husband will often say to me "you look at life through rose colored glasses." To which I respond, "you should get a pair, it makes life much more enjoyable!"

Dr. Wayne Dyer wrote many books about our ability to change our lives by simply changing our thoughts. One of my favorite quotes from him is "change the way you look at things and the things you look at change." To me, this quote is all about perception, and our ability to shift our perceptions to change the landscape of our lives. I've been amazed at how powerful a simple shift can be when it comes to reshaping my mindset. When I ask myself "how can I see this differently?," I force myself to think of alternatives and actively search for a better, more positive feeling.

When it comes to perfectionism, we can choose to give up the need to be perfect or to compare ourselves to others and simply find joy where we are in the present moment. When I find myself falling into the rabbit hole of comparison, I remind myself that comparison is the thief of joy. I tell myself to run my own race and not worry about what others are doing or thinking.

And when I recognize that I am caught in the loop of not yet good enough (like right now while I'm writing and rewriting this chapter), I stop and ask myself "Have you done your best? And are you allowing perfect to be the enemy of done?" And I remind myself that sometimes good has to be good enough!

One of my favorite quotes about perfectionism comes from Dr. Brene Brown. She says "perfectionism is the 20 ton shield we carry around to try to protect ourselves from being hurt, but it actually protects us from being seen." She says fear is at the root of perfectionism, and that protectionists are afraid that the world will see them for who they really are and they won't measure up.

The most important lesson when it comes to perfectionism (and this is one that I'm still learning) is that we have nothing to prove and there's no need to impress others. This eliminates the external drivers of perfectionism. We need to remember that life is all about learning and growing. It's not about being perfect!

The truth is, none of us is perfect. We all have issues and things we'd like to improve. We all feel less than perfect at times, and often feel as though we are not good enough. But we are all doing the best we can. And we are ALL "enough!"

Thought-Provoking, Self-Reflection Questions:
1. What does perfection mean to you?
2. How is perfectionism holding you back in life?
3. What could you do with the time you save by giving up the need to be perfect?

_____

_____

_____

_____

_____

_____

_____

_____

_____

_____

_____

_____

_____

_____

_____

_____

_____

_____

_____

_____

_____

_____

_____

_____

_____

Chapter 11 - Regret

Dr. Carol Minski
President, CMA Leadership Consultants

> *"Regret is a very serious topic because it has to do a lot of times with perception. Personally I try to live without regret. So don't have regrets, turn them into a wish. Think about the end of your life and what you wish you would have accomplished and then add a goal to that and you won't have regrets."*

Nancy Werteen:

I can see her like it was yesterday but it was nearly 30 years ago. All these years later, there is her tiny limp body dangling in a police officer's arms. Her long brown hair jostling furiously as he ran to a waiting ambulance that couldn't help her. Too late, they said. As a young reporter, your first fatality is like a rite of passage. You never forget.

Her mom was driving out to the Hamptons from Manhattan. Busy Friday afternoon. Summertime. Traffic was awful. She was hot, stressed and tired. Her little girl didn't want to be in her car seat anymore. And her tiny Yorkie kept running around the car. Was so irritating. Mom made a decision. She'd strap the dog in the car seat and let her daughter out. Just for a few minutes. Give everyone a break. And then it happened. A terrible collision.

As I watched the Yorkie gleefully running around the accident scene, happy to meet new people, I was sick to my stomach. Not a scratch on him.

Please tell me how that mom lives with THAT regret. How does anyone?

I think we all have something in our lives we've done or didn't do that we regret-that we wish we'd done differently-that we wish never happened. We all have those times when one split second decision could have or did change everything. But we didn't know the outcome. And if we did, we would have acted differently.

I love this quote from Maya Angelou: "Do the best you can until you know better. Then when you know better, do better." That's all any of us can really do. My dad is in his early 80's now and I find he ruminates on regret. He will shake his head thinking about decisions he made as a firefighter. He'll talk about a certain fire and say, "Why did I turn right? I should have turned left and I would have found that kid before it was too late." In his day, firefighters just went into burning buildings. They didn't wait to put on a breathing apparatus. They just went in and used sheer determination, muscle and instinct to make a rescue. The walls of my parent's den are lined with pictures of him holding children, men, women and pets, all of them covered in soot and fear. I tell him to focus on those images, but he's still haunted by the people he couldn't save. Tells me they keep him up at night. He's working through it and understands that he probably should have had some help after particularly tragic events, but that wasn't how things were done back then.

I'm thankful he talks to me about it sometimes. It's a burden he shouldn't have to carry. Regret can be like that-a 200 pound weight you carry on your back. But at some point, you have to come to terms with your decisions. I think regret can destroy people.

My guess is we all have some cringeworthy thing lurking inside our minds that we regret. I know I have mine. But I won't mention it. Thinking I've given you enough disturbing images for one chapter. The trick is to understand your limitations at the time and your true intentions. And while the end of that poor little girl's life continues in the strange nooks and crannies that is my memory storage, I pray her mother has let her regrets go. I pray she's allowed herself to take that awful burden off her shoulders.

Look in anyone's soul and you have to believe there is good intention there. It just gets mixed up with things like circumstances, distraction and ego. And like a recipe that mixes ingredients that just taste awful together, sometimes the outcome leaves a bad taste in our mouths.

But in the end, you have to let it go. You know better now, so you can do better next time.

Kim Howie:

Holding on to regret is essentially living your life in the past. One thing I know for sure is that we can't go back in time and change things that have already happened. We can, however, reframe the way we choose to see those experiences and use those lessons to make better decisions in the future. This involves self-reflection.

It's tempting to try to offload the blame onto others when we feel regretful. However, taking responsibility for our actions enables us to own our power to either make amends or learn from our mistakes. Placing blame on others may alleviate our guilt, but it only replaces that guilt with anger, which is just another emotion that does not serve us in the end.

Self-reflection allows us to step back and look at the situation with an open mind and an open heart. Recognizing that the choices we made led us down a path we did not want. One solution is to ask ourselves if there's a way to see things differently. Maybe this path isn't as bad as we have made it out to be. Maybe we needed to take one step backward in order to take two steps forward. Another solution is to ask, "how can I make amends?" What needs to be done or said to begin the process of rebuilding? This helps us shift to become solution focused rather than ruminating on the problem.

After we've reframed the experience through self-reflection and processed through the subsequent emotions, the next step is to let go. One of my favorite lines to say to my children is "I've let that go." They tease me and say I use that as an excuse to cover up for the things I've forgotten. This may be partially true, but I often make the conscious choice to let go of things that I know are not serving me. It's easy to ruminate on things that we wish we had done differently. But the truth is obsessing about the past won't change anything. And holding on to regret is painful. Choosing to let things go allows us to move forward without guilt or resentment. It's a valuable skill that takes practice and time to master.

Another important tool when it comes to regret is self-compassion. We need to let ourselves off the hook and turn our forgiveness inward. Forgiving ourselves is often harder than forgiving others. The first step is recognizing that the negative self-talk is not helping us in any way. Remember, we're all human and therefore we will make mistakes. Recognizing our shared humanity and knowing that others have made the same or similar mistakes can also be helpful. Next we need to speak gently to ourselves, the way a wise and caring friend would respond if we told them about our regret. Self-compassion is a skill that requires practice and persistence. But when mastered, it is truly life changing.

Personally, I think the worst kinds of regrets are the ones where you wished you had done, said or tried something, but you allowed fear to hold you back. Don't allow that kind of regret to happen to you! Go out and live your life, don't hold back, live, laugh, and love out loud!

Thought-Provoking, Self-Reflection Questions:
1. What regrets are you holding on to?
2. How can you look at those situations differently?
3. Actively let go of them NOW!

_____

_____

_____

_____

_____

_____

_____

_____

_____

_____

_____

_____

_____

_____

_____

_____

_____

_____

_____

_____

_____

_____

_____

_____

_____

Chapter 12 - Love

Beth Songer
Trauma and Addictions counselor

"I think everything we do, every thought, every feeling, each perception, our consciousness, is a call for love, especially to love ourselves, because I think when we feel regret, feel mistakes, when we shame ourselves as a failure, it's because we don't accept ourselves as we are."

Nancy Werteen:

I remember the first guy who ever broke my heart-sort of. I was just out of high school. He had an Italian sounding last name and a hunter green Corvette. He said if things worked out he'd have me over to his house one Sunday for his mother's sauce. A few years older than me, he had a job and took me to restaurants and ordered shrimp cocktail and filet mignon, which seemed so exotic to me. One day, he announced that he was breaking up with me. What? "Why?" I asked. "What did I do?" "Nothing," he said. "I just don't love you." Just like that. I wasn't his cup of tea. He dropped me off at my house and I somehow got out of the car in my stunned silence. In the house, I stood there, key in hand. He didn't love me. The pain of this statement and realization just slammed me in the gut like a baseball bat. I literally threw up. Being 17 or 18 or whatever I was, I spent days in my bedroom crying and arguing with my mom and my friends that I would absolutely never get over it. He and his Corvette were all I ever wanted. Yeah, right. I can't even remember his name or what he looked like anymore! But I do remember how much being rejected hurt and I really did want to taste his mother's homemade sauce. And looking back, I think "I just don't love you" was actually code for, "you're not putting out so I am out of here."

But seriously, love is like magic isn't it? When you have it, you feel like you can conquer the world. Every fiber of your being seems electrified. Colors are brighter and sweets taste somehow even sweeter. And when it goes away, the music stops doesn't it? Not long after Mr. Green Corvette, I took up with another character with an Italian sounding last name but this time I didn't feel the spark. This time I was the one who walked away, sure I would suffocate if I stayed. What is it that attracts us to another person? At that point in my life, I think it was just a feeling of how great it felt to be chosen, to know someone thought I could be the one.

When I first started dating my husband some ten years later, we were both very clear about who we were and what we wanted. Now don't get me wrong, we were attracted to each other for the typical reasons you notice someone. He was frankly hot as hell and I couldn't get enough of him. Our eyes would lock if we were in the same room with an intensity that made me hold my breath. If he was there, it seemed like no one else was in the room. We actually started talking about marriage just a few months in. And the most ridiculous part is that I came to Allentown "just for a few months." Never even took the New York plates off my car. But there was something about him. I had had my share of boyfriends by this point but no one reached in and held my heart the way he does. He has a enthusiasm for life that's so attractive and contagious. I always say when he gets to the pearly gates, he'll bungee cord in to meet Saint Pete with a smile on his face excited for the next adventure. On our second date, we found ourselves in a firehouse (long story) and even though he was working hard to impress me, he was compelled to put on the turnout gear of one of the firefighter's, which weighs about 45 pounds, so he could run around the firehouse just to "experience how it would feel." I was smitten.

His proposal was a surprise. We worked together back then and he got down on one knee at a company party, television cameras rolling. This was 25 years ago, pre-social media and iPhones. But you don't work in a television station and not record these things.

I remember when we passed the 18-year mark. We turned to each other with the realization we had lived together longer than we had lived with our parents. I love that I know what he's going to say before he even says it. I love that he will tell me what I'm about to say. He pushes me, he challenges me, he compliments me, sometimes he pisses me off. And I'm sure I irritate him sometimes, although I can't imagine how. Our love has gone through changes and stages and challenges, but we always remind each other we are in it for the long haul. We remind each other why together we're better, why we are the half of a whole. We laugh, we cry, we reminisce. When I look at him, I still feel that pull, that energy, that glue that keeps us together. He's smart and funny and looks the same to me as he did all those years ago. When he enters a room now, I feel him before I even see him. I can pick his gait out of a thousand people on the darkest night. This love, a true love, evolves over time and it's not always neat and perfect. In fact, it can be downright messy. But like the seasons, there's a certainty to it that's just as exciting as the early days of long gazes and awkward comments.

The gifts we give each other can't be measured in any sort of literal capacity. They are endless. I look forward to what's next in our continuing life together with a realization that I'm blessed, lucky even to have such a strong bond. That's love and the most traditional sense of the word love I guess.

When we look at our lives, we really are surrounded by love. Our family, friends, co-workers, children, even our pets bring the light of love into our lives every day. One night not too long ago, I was texting Kim after a few cocktails. Defenses down, I casually wrote, "I love you." Knowing me, after she wrote how thrilled she was that I said that (that's what you have to know about her) she wrote, "I love you too and now you can't take it back!" She knew I would panic and try to. Why can't we say we love another person with abandon like that? Why does it make us so uncomfortable to admit it? I do love her for Heaven's sake. And what's wrong with that?

To have love is to be alive, truly alive. But I think we don't celebrate it enough. I know I don't. I feel like we should tell the people we love that we love them and tell them often with enthusiasm. I guess it's not part of normal social graces. I'm already in a panic and wondering if I should take that part out about loving Kim! But I think I'll leave it in. It's put a smile on my face and I'm sure it will have her doing the same.

Kim Howie:

Experts say there are two main types of love, passionate and compassionate love. We all know what passionate love is, it's that heart-pumping dizzy feeling we have when we are overcome by attraction to another person. But compassionate love is more subtle and steady by nature. It is unconditional and can be exuded towards any living creature. It is said to be one of the main keys to inner peace and wellbeing.

Compassionate love is comprised of companionship and friendship along with a feeling of connection to others. Authentic connection is at the root of all loving relationships. It's what we are ALL truly seeking in life ~ a feeling of love and belonging.

Being in any type of a loving relationship, whether it's passionate or compassionate love, requires you to be vulnerable, which means letting others see your authentic self. It also involves self-disclosure and a willingness to be open and honest about your deepest feelings. It can be difficult to express love for others, especially if we fear that our feelings either won't be reciprocated or will make the other person feel uncomfortable.

I have to say that Nancy's right (as usual); I had a big smile on my face after reading her recount of the time she texted me to say, "I love you." Of course I knew in my heart that she did, but to read the text, especially knowing how closely Nancy keeps her emotions hidden, was a real gift! Sometimes we aren't aware of how powerful our words can be, and the impact it makes when we share our true feelings with another.

Personally, I've always been a big fan of sharing my feelings, and I truly love when others share their feelings with me; but I do understand that there are people who struggle with opening up and letting others in. So I like to remind myself of the "platinum rule:" treat others as THEY want to be treated (rather than the golden rule where you treat others as YOU want to be treated.) And keep in mind that you can express love through actions as well as words.

Several years ago I read a wonderful book called *The Five Love Languages* written by Dr. Gary Chapman. In the book he outlines the five general ways he found that most people like to express and receive love. This was really life changing for me and my family, as I could see that we each had a different love language and I needed to make sure that I was speaking the right language when I was sharing my love with my husband and my children.

Here is a brief overview of the five love languages:

1. Words of Affirmation ~ giving praise to your loved one. Verbal compliments.
2. Quality Time ~ spending time together. Giving your undivided attention.
3. Receiving Gifts ~ getting physical or emotional gifts. Receiving tokens of love.
4. Acts of Service ~ doing something nice for your loved one. Seeking to please.
5. Physical Touch ~ skin to skin contact.

And here is a summary of how to speak each of them:

Words of Affirmation

Those who have words of affirmation as their primary love language feel most loved when they receive compliments and encouraging words from others. These can be simple compliments such as "you look great" or "I'm really proud of you." Or they can be statements of recognition including the person's strengths or accomplishments, such as "Your article was really well written; I can tell that you put a lot of effort into it." Besides making us feel good, these words of affirmation can help to build us up and unleash potential that may otherwise remain dormant.

Words of Affirmation is my primary love language, so I know the power that it holds for me personally. When my husband compliments me or says encouraging words about me or my work, my whole world lights up and I feel truly loved. Yet, although like most people my husband enjoys being complimented, he doesn't need those words of affirmation to feel loved. This realization was an important one for both of us!

Quality Time

Those who have quality time as their preferred love language feel most loved when they have regularly scheduled time together with their loved ones doing things they enjoy. During this time, it's important that they are given undivided attention. This may seem obvious and easy, but we are living in an era of information overload, where it's difficult to focus 100% of our attention on anything or anyone for even a moment much less an extended period of time. Oftentimes we are moving through life at light speed simply trying to keep all of our balls up in the air. However, when it comes to providing others with quality time, we must stop the stream of incoming mental media and focus ALL of our attention on the present moment.

Chapman explains that quality time involves quality activities and quality conversation, meaning sharing our feelings with one another. He says that effective sharing and listening are equally important when it comes to staying connected to each other. Unfortunately, it's rare to have a conversation with someone who actually listens to what we're saying without interruption or judgment. We all want to be heard, and true connection can only occur when people listen to each other. By harnessing the power of listening, we can greatly improve the quality of our communication and our relationships. When in conversation, Chapman says we should try to concentrate and listen to what the other person is saying, and while they are speaking, put all thoughts out of our head and be present for them. This takes practice and awareness. Chapman says that quality time doesn't necessarily mean spending a long period of uninterrupted time together, but rather making the time spent together meaningful and attentive.

Receiving Gifts

Those who have receiving gifts as their primary love language view gifts as a visual symbol of love. Dr. Chapman says "a gift is something you can hold in your hand and say 'look, he was thinking of me,' or 'she remembered me.' And the gift is a symbol of that thought."

Giving tangible gifts doesn't necessarily mean that we need to spend a lot of money; however, according to Dr. Chapman, if we are to become effective gift givers, we may need to change our attitude about money. Chapman notes that if we are spenders by nature, then purchasing gifts will likely not be difficult for us; however, if we are savers, we may experience emotional resistance to the idea of spending money, even if it is as an expression of love. He says if money is an issue, we can make gifts that come from the heart, and we can also give the intangible gifts of our time and attention, as these don't cost anything, and oftentimes are worth more than the tangible gifts!

Acts of Service

Acts of service means doing things that we know will make others happy. This could include making a meal, cleaning the house or servicing the car. When our loved one has acts of service as their primary love language, it's important to realize that doing simple things like picking up their dry cleaning can result in them feeling loved, and on the flipside, when we don't do things for them, they may interpret that to mean that we don't love them as much.

This was a great insight for my daughters. One of them has the primary love language of physical touch, while the other has acts of service. When they learned to speak each other's love language, our household became much more harmonious. Prior to that time, when my youngest (physical touch) would try to show my oldest (acts of service) that she loved her, she would run up and give her a big hug. When her physical affection did not receive a warm welcome, she felt unloved. However, when she started pitching in and helping her sister with chores (acts of service ~ which made her older sister feel loved), she was rewarded with gratitude (and sometimes even a hug ~ physical touch), which in turn made her feel loved.

Physical Touch

It feels good to be touched, to be massaged, and to feel physically connected to other people. Dr. Chapman says, "to a person whose primary love language is physical touch, the message of a hug is far louder than words."

When it comes to physical touch, a little can go a long way, and physical touch can have a positive impact on your relationship and your health. But society sometimes confuses touching with sexuality, and this is why some people live in fear of touch. Touching can sometimes make people feel uncomfortable because it is an open expression of love, care, and appreciation. If that's the case for you, don't worry, just be honest and start an open dialog so you can break through this by finding a comfortable non-threatening way to connect.

You may find that you enjoy speaking (and being spoken to) in many or all of these love languages, but research shows that we typically have a primary love language. Keep in mind that there is no judgment in the process of identifying your love language. None is better than the others. This is not a tool to help you find fault in yourself or in others; it's simply a way to identify and communicate the way in which you feel most loved.

Using the love languages as a tool can be a fun way to get to know yourself and your loved ones better. Recognizing that our perceptions of what others want may be different than what they really want. The best way to know for sure is to ask them!

Thought-Provoking, Self-Reflection Questions:
1. Do you have difficulty expressing or receiving love?
2. What is your primary love language?
3. How can you communicate that to your partner?

_____

_____

_____

_____

_____

_____

_____

_____

_____

_____

_____

_____

_____

_____

_____

_____

_____

_____

_____

_____

_____

_____

_____

_____

_____

Chapter 13 - Trust/Betrayal:

Pam Deller
Magazine Publisher, Lehigh Valley Style

> *"There are definitely times I have been betrayed and times I*
> *have betrayed. I think you have to know that that is going to*
> *happen to you in life, that you're going to trust in someone*
> *that you shouldn't have or sometimes you're going to do*
> *something stupid and hurt somebody you didn't mean to."*

Nancy Werteen:

Good Lord this is a hard one. Betrayal is so difficult and I frankly can't think of anything funny to say about it. So I'll start with trust. Why in the world do we make the choice to trust or not to trust another person? What do we base it on? Something someone said or how they look or act? Is that really all there is to it? I remember reading a book about Ted Bundy. Remember him? Serial killer who used to stalk girls on college campuses. He'd put on a fake cast or use crutches or something like that and ask an unsuspecting girl for help. The unfortunate ones trusted him. Why? He was handsome, clean cut, seemed like a regular guy. I think we learn to trust or not trust based on our life and our circumstances which go back to our childhood.

I remember the taste of a just right summer peach. There was a peach farm on the way back from the beach. Growing up on Long Island, just about everything is "on the way back from the beach." We would stop and my mom would buy a basket of peaches. I'd choose one, bite down and watch the peach juice drip down my hands and land on my sand covered feet. To this day when I eat a warm summer peach, it feels like home. It's interesting how a smell or a taste can transport you to another time and place. So many things you remember and so many things you forget. I think we learn to trust in the things that are constant. After an experience, we measure what was true and what wasn't and then we learn to trust in our instincts and in the people around us.

And at some point, we make a mistake. We trust something or someone that we shouldn't have. When I was 15, I used to swing on a tire swing at my friend's house. Higher and higher we'd go. We trusted it would stay nailed into that tree. Well one day, it didn't. Higher and higher I went until the nail came loose and I flew across the backyard landing in the emergency room. We trust and then we become more careful. No more tire swings for me after that. Actually, I don't even like swings at all. Of course that's a metaphor for life and relationships. We trust until we are betrayed and then, well then we don't trust so easily anymore. And sometimes we can't even trust ourselves.

I thought I'd never forget the first ten words my daughter said. Figured I didn't even have to write them down, I'd always remember. But I don't. And then there are awful things I remember and can't forget. It seems we don't always get to choose what stays and what goes. I suppose there are good and bad things about that. The past can be a wrecking ball or a soft kiss on a warm summer day. We have all been betrayed in many ways, situations and circumstances.

The key seems to be recognizing that we aren't at fault when someone doesn't live up to the expectations that we have for them. And don't even get me going on that subject. I think so many of our disappointments come because we aren't clear about what we want or what we expect. Sometimes we come up with these grand ideas for what we think a certain relationship or experience will be like but we don't share that with the other people involved. And when they don't live up to our expectations, we blame them. Is it really their fault or our own fault?

We are human and we trust. We have to. We have to trust that there are things and people we can rely on or we would be too scared to even get out of bed in the morning. But trusting someone should come with a disclaimer: *The following person is only human and flawed and may in fact not be completely trustworthy in every situation you are giving him or her credit for.* Might not take the sting of betrayal completely away, but it could soften the blow a little bit. Betrayal sucks plain and simple. But if I've learned nothing else in my life, I know that I have to let those things go for my own sake. Feel it and forget it as best you can.

Kim Howie:

I've always thought of trust as though it's similar to innocence in the court of law (you're innocent until proven guilty); I trust you until you prove you're not trustworthy. I am a sharer by nature, as authentic connection is important to me. Over the course of my life, this has come to burn me at times where I've shared something with someone assuming they were trustworthy only to later find out that they weren't. I think we can probably all relate to that. The trick becomes not allowing that betrayal to close your heart to sharing with others in the future.

Dr. Brene Brown shares an acronym she created to describe the necessary components for trust in her book, *Rising Strong.* This acronym is BRAVING. I love acronyms and this one in particular has great value and significant meaning. The acronym breaks down like this:

B ~ boundaries

R ~ reliability

A ~ accountability

V ~ vault

I ~ integrity

N ~ nonjudgment

G ~ generosity

I won't share personal details on all of the letters, but I want to share my reflections on the ones that I find to be the most significant in my life. Reliability is really important to me. I find that if I can rely on a person to follow through and do what they say, I am more likely to trust them. And I work hard to do the same in return. I hold myself accountable to the commitments I make to people, and if I can't follow through, I make amends. That goes for accountability as well. This is a big one for me. It's so important to take responsibility for our actions, especially when they are at the root of something that went wrong. Trust breaks down when people displace blame onto others. I've done a lot of personal work in this area over the last several years. I started to notice that I had a tendency to find a scapegoat for my mistakes. Even silly things like if I tripped and dropped a dish while walking across the floor. I'd immediately look to push the blame off on my children for leaving their things on the floor and causing me to trip, rather than taking responsibility for my lack of mindfulness while walking. It's really easy to blame others for our actions or our current situation, but in doing so, we give up our personal power. When we take responsibility for our actions, we put ourselves back in control of our lives and our self-efficacy. That reminds me of another wonderful quote I love from Dr. Brown which is "when we own our story, we get to write the ending."

As for the BRAVING acronym, I think the biggest one for me is the vault. This means that what I tell you stays locked up in a vault, not to be shared with others. Again, this goes both ways, if I'm going to trust that you won't share things I've disclosed to you in confidence, I need to reciprocate in the same manner. I can recall several decades ago being flabbergasted when I found out that some discord in my personal life was part of the rumor mill at my place of employment. It took some time and some personal introspection for me to realize that prior to that time I had happily participated in fueling that same rumor mill with personal information about other people's lives. Sometimes life turns the tables on us to teach us a valuable lesson. I got that one loud and clear!

What I love most about Dr. Brene Brown's acronym is that the root word is brave, as we really do need to be brave in order to trust people! We also have to recognize that other people are being brave when they trust us. Trust is a two-way street. We can't expect trust from others if we don't trust them in return. We also can't expect others to trust us if we can't trust ourselves or act in a trustworthy way.

As for betrayal, this is a hard lesson to learn in life. But I also think that it provides dichotomy. Sometimes we need to be on the receiving end of betrayal to recognize what it feels like and know that we don't ever want to do that to anyone else.

I recently took the time to write down my personal values. I look at them often and hold myself accountable to them. Being trustworthy is one of those values. It's one that I aspire to achieve each and every day. Being kind, compassionate, and nonjudgmental are some of the others. When my actions are not in alignment with those values, I make amends and vow to do better next time. And I try to remember that we are here to grow from our experiences, and none of us is perfect!

Thought-Provoking, Self-Reflection Questions:
1. Who do you trust the most in life?
2. Are there people in your life that have shaken your trust?
3. Is there someone you betrayed that you need to make amends or a betrayal that you need to let go?

_____

_____

_____

_____

_____

_____

_____

_____

_____

_____

_____

_____

_____

_____

_____

_____

_____

_____

_____

_____

_____

Chapter 14 - Passion and Purpose

Caroline Bitterly
Lafayette College Student

"I never fully understood passion until I experienced the power of the human connection, and the inexplicable joy that it brings. Passion is the energy that fuels us when we discover connectivity in all aspects of our life. When you feel truly connected... to people, to your career, to the ambiance surrounding you — that's something you will be passionate about. You will want to keep this feeling in your everyday life. So passion is really the discovery and the becoming of a person. Once I found my passion, I essentially found myself. "

Nancy Werteen:

Now don't get all fired up. Passion doesn't mean we're suddenly shifting to the Fifty Shades of Grey version of our project. We're talking here about the passion you feel for life, for people, for experiences and for challenges. Years ago, I covered a news story about an older couple who owned a farm. He, a mimic of Santa with a white beard, and she, his trusty side kick, with a warm smile and a hug for everyone. This was somewhere around 1994 when HIV and AIDS had a frightening grip on our country. These folks must have been upper 60s or early 70s, I'm guessing. They had eight foster children-all with full blown HIV. This couple told me they felt a child should have a pony, especially a child who was dying. And so on this farm were eight children who each paraded a pony out for us to see. Talk about passion. Even though this couple wasn't in the best of health themselves, they told me this gift was their purpose, their reason for living. And it was easy to see that they got as much as they gave. The children seemed happy, even if the farm was simple and they had to share rooms and hand-me-down clothes. They were loved and each one had a pony. A dream come true. There was no sadness. No mention of the death sentence that hung over each of their heads. Love seemed to burst from the interactions between them all. I didn't want to leave.

That kind of passion for anything is contagious, isn't it? We see the fulfillment and sheer joy in someone who brims with excitement for a cause or an idea and many of us will feel a tug to be part of it too, to have a piece of that kind of dedication. We all want that passion, we just have to find it. For me, that road has been long and pretty convoluted.

In my early teens, I volunteered to be a candy striper at a local Catholic hospital. We wore these red and white striped jumpers with white short sleeved collared shirts underneath. Ever see those? I'm dating myself again but this was the mid-70s I guess, pre-HIPAA and tons of other rules and regulations. So even though we were volunteers, by today's standards, you would never have guessed it. My friend and I went every Sunday for three years. We'd start at 9:00am and would wrap up around 5:00pm. There was a nurse in charge of us girls and we'd all go up to whatever unit she assigned us to and begin our work. First, we got each patient out of bed and into a chair. Then, ready for this? WE changed the bed sheets, the bed pans, replaced the chucks, cleaned up whatever fluids were on the floor and went to the next room. The nurses trained and trusted us and went on to more important things. Sometimes, they told us they'd handle a certain room or patient who was too medically fragile but for the most part, we did the heavy lifting. After changing all the linens, and it usually took a good couple of hours, the lunch trays were delivered on huge carts. We went room to room, delivering a lunch tray to each person and feeding the patients who needed help eating. By then, it was around 1:00pm and we proceeded to the chapel to clean and polish the pews after morning mass.

Even though it was hard work, I loved it, mostly when we were lucky enough to get an hour or two in the ER. The chaos and the pace thrilled me. That gurney would slam through the entrance way and I couldn't wait to see what would happen next. In the ER, we were just support services. Someone would yell, "Candy striper-get water" or "Candy striper-clean linens!" One time a nurse grabbed my arm and pulled me to a woman sitting in a chair. The nurse looked me in the face with that stern look adults give kids and she said, "Comfort her." I gingerly sat down next to the woman who had a huge black eye, tears on her face, mucus coming out of her nose. When I sat next to her, she just started talking. "He didn't mean it, really. Sometimes he just gets like this. It's my fault. I should have made something better for dinner…" And on and on she went. It finally dawned on me what is probably obvious to you. Her husband had beat the crap out of her. A neighbor pulled him off and pummeled the husband within an inch of his life. While doctors frantically tried to save his physical body, the woman worked desperately to save his reputation, talking to anyone who would listen. Even me. I must have sat with her for three or four hours. I didn't really understand then but I knew she needed someone and at that moment, that someone was me.

Those years and that hospital had a huge impact on me. It was the first time in my life that people treated me like an adult, not just a kid. I learned to speak to adults, to follow directions, to clean up my mistakes. I learned that a warm touch and a kind word could mean so much to another person. Sometimes we'd just sit with a patient, especially on the geriatric ward. So many people scared and lonely. I'd leave that hospital and hit the fresh air outside with a renewed vigor for life.

Now when it came to high school graduation, I couldn't make things easy. I decided to buck the system and figured I wasn't going to go to college "just because everyone else was doing it." Hmmm...yeah... sounds like an 18-year-old. At 6'1", living close to Manhattan, I decided I would be discovered as a model in New York City. Like it's that easy! But this was my grand plan so I set off with the determination only a teenager can have. I worked in an office three days a week and went on casting calls the other two. After a year of getting myself into situations that still make me cringe, one day I threw my modeling portfolio into a trash can after another sleazy agent made a pass at me, this time trying to literally suck my toes after saying he had been searching for a foot model.

After that, I swallowed my pride and decided to go to college. I turned back to what I thought was my passion. Nursing, I figured. My mom is from a long line of doctors and she and I were fired up for me to follow the medical path. I did a year of courses like anatomy and physiology and had literally hundreds of post-it notes on my bathroom mirror and wall-and I still know that the thoracic cavity is subdivided into pleural cavities-but then I took an elective. Journalism. Wow!!! I couldn't wait to get to class. When the professor assigned a paper, I'd do three. When he told us to do an original interview, I went to a nightclub and interviewed a male stripper. Hey, I was 19 by then, that's what I was interested in! The professor said my writing needed work but he was really surprised by my choice of subject matter. "Adventurous," he said. "I love it!" I would tell my mom how much I couldn't wait to go to that class and I blathered on about who I could interview next. She reminded me about how as a little kid, maybe 10, I would follow her around the house asking for a title of a story. She'd make something up to get me out of her hair and I'd hunker down in a corner to write my masterpiece.

She and I didn't know what I could do with a journalism degree but she said if it speaks to me, I should follow my heart. So I did. It wasn't long after heading down that road that I found television and I could see how everything in my past had led me to that point. My path became quite clear after that.

And then life throws you a curveball doesn't it? For me, after 14 years on the anchor desk, I stepped away because I found my passion in a sweet baby girl I couldn't live without. Our passions change and morph at times I guess. And people can be our passion too. My husband, my family, my children: people become our reasons for living.

How terribly awful it would be to not be passionate about anything. What is that saying? That the opposite of love isn't hate; it's indifference. It's not caring. Not giving a shit. What an empty existence that would be. Right now, I'm passionate about my family, still television, writing and The Wisdom Coalition, among other things. Passion is the fuel for survival we all need. Step back. Remember your passions and light them on fire with the largest flame you can find. I'll be right there with you. We'll heat up together. Okay, now I'm getting back to the R-rated version of passion, but at least I've got your attention!!

Kim Howie:

To me, purpose and meaning are terms that define the reason we exist and the why behind everything that we do and everything that happens in life. I believe that purpose and meaning are driving forces that come from within. Meaning is personal and unique for each of us and is brought into focus through awareness. I also believe that meaning provides hope and guides our choices in life. When we understand the reason for life experiences, we are better able to apply the lessons to help us make better choices for ourselves in the future.

I have vacillated back and forth over the question of what gives my life meaning. I will sometimes think that the roles I play (wife, mother, daughter, sister, Health Coach, business owner, friend, etc.) give my life meaning; yet other times I believe that we are so much more than what we do in life. In this way, meaning in my life is more about growth and expansion for my soul. Therefore, God forbid something tragic were to happen and I lost some or all of my roles, my life would still have meaning.

I believe that we are all on a journey, and we find ourselves taking turns along the way that have an impact on the direction in which we are traveling. My life has taken several turns that could be described as "wrong turns," but I choose to see them as opportunities to have learned important lessons about life, love, and taking responsibility for my own actions.

Up until about 5 years ago, I hadn't thought much about whether my life had any significant meaning or purpose. I was just reacting to whatever came my way. Then one day I began to realize that I actually could play an active role in my own life, and make choices that could have significant impact on my overall wellbeing. This was the beginning of my spiritual journey. This was when life took on a whole new meaning.

I started down the path of self discovery and along the way connected with my inner self, my soul. I began to realize that life is truly what I make of it, and that I create my own reality by choosing where I want to place my attention. I suddenly felt empowered, but even more so, I felt connected to myself, to others, and to life.

As for passion, I think you know it when you feel it! It's not something you seek, but rather something that finds you! For me, I know that I'm lit up with passion when I get goosebumps when I think about or hear about something that speaks to my soul. I remember when Nancy and I were just starting The Wisdom Coalition. It was "our project" and I was filled with passion every time I thought about a new idea or concept related to it. Ideas were coming to me in dreams and interrupting my meditation sessions, and suddenly I'd be covered in goosebumps!

I remember hearing once that goosebumps are a sign from your inner-being that you are in alignment with your true self. This makes sense to me as I still get goosebumps when I think about the work we do at The Wisdom Coalition. It's my passion and purpose to help others find joy and peace in life; and doing this work brings me tremendous joy, which I believe is the ultimate meaning and purpose of life.

Thought-Provoking, Self-Reflection Questions:
1. What are you passionate about?
2. What do you feel is the purpose of your life?
3. How do you define the meaning of life?

_____

_____

_____

_____

_____

_____

_____

_____

_____

_____

_____

_____

_____

_____

_____

_____

_____

_____

_____

_____

_____

_____

_____

_____

_____

_____

Chapter 15 - Your Legacy

Gladys Wiles
Attorney
President, Snyder & Wiles

"I think what I would want to leave, my gift to the world is to impart to my children the ability to live life to the fullest. Laugh at whatever is funny to them. Love everything around them and as much as possible and I think that causes a ripple effect so if you're putting it out to the world and you have others putting it out there hopefully it has an impact on those that surround us and I think that would be a nice legacy to leave."

Nancy Werteen:

Working in television news, it's really hard not to get cynical. You see the absolute worst in people. Yes, you see the best too but not nearly as often. A wife goes missing and the husband appears on camera swearing he had nothing to do with it and we in the newsroom turn to each other and say, "yeah, he did it." The politician promises and we snicker. The public relations expert spins and we look for what's hiding. We know the way we speak in the newsroom is not normal and so we temper our words when other people are around but for the most part, we look for the worst and hope for the best in most situations.

Now this attitude hasn't always made me the most easy going parent. The first time I dropped my older daughter alone at the movies, she must have been 13 or so, before letting her and her buddy out of the car, I said, "Listen you two. Don't you dare buy a ticket to the movie we agreed on and then sneak into an R-rated movie." They both looked at me with blank faces. "Why would we do that?" She asked. Course I had just done a story on this very thing, so I told her that. She rolled her eyes as any self-respecting teenager would do and said, "Why can't you just be a normal mom?" Sorry my dear, you drew the short straw on that one.

With a job that consists of being pounded over the head by the evils of the world, it can be paralyzing to face that world on your time off, especially when your children walk into it. Thinking back to all those stories I've covered in my almost 30-year career, unfortunately, it's mostly the nasty ones I remember. I can rattle off about a dozen criminal cases off the top of my head with names and heinous details of suffering and death. There are people who have built a legacy with building blocks of evil deeds and that's what they're remembered for.

Why is a legacy so important anyway? Walk through a graveyard and you'll see "beloved wife" or "devoted father." We want to be remembered. At work, in our families, most of us hope when our name is mentioned, there's a fond remembrance that settles over the conversation. "Oh, she is so nice." or "I learned so much from him." In newsrooms, we don't report on suicides out of respect for the person who made that awful decision, but also for anyone who might want to do the same. No sense bringing attention to it. Politicians talk about a legacy but most of us don't really actively think about it until we're older. But now that I've mentioned it, I bet your wheels are spinning and you're wondering what your legacy might be. And that's a good thing-to take a look at who you are and who you want to be.

When my older daughter was going through a particularly difficult age when your parents are the most embarrassing people in the world, she hated shopping with me. She actually insisted that we text only. No speaking allowed. Me, trying to be the understanding mom, went along with this insanity. We'd walk through the mall and pass a rack of swim suits. I would text her, "Do you like the blue one?" or something like that.

Infuriating. At this time I was dragging along my younger one who loved to play in the dressing rooms and couldn't wait to crawl underneath from one room to the next. Didn't get a lot of actual purchasing done in those days. Anyway, this one particular trip, the little one had to pee and I was having a hot flash carrying all the coats and then the nonsense "Do you like this" texting and I blew a gasket. "That's it!" I wailed. "Can't we just speak?" I had broken the cardinal rule. I actually spoke to her in the store. Now, she was mortified and really mad and wouldn't answer me with words or a text. Then I really blew. "Out to the car NOW." Once there, she was all in a huff and I was fuming. So this is the question I come up with. "Alright, what's so embarrassing about me?" Talk about setting yourself up for a disaster. She looked at me, exhaled loudly and said, "Well...you could be like 10 years younger!" I swallowed that and followed up. "That's the best you've got?" We held each other's gaze for what seemed like forever and then I noticed the side of her mouth turn up ever so slightly. Her eyes softened. I felt my mouth start to spread. And then it happened. We burst out laughing. We laughed harder than we had in months both realizing the ridiculousness of our questions, our answers and the situation.

I like to tell that story. We still laugh about it. I wonder if it's now part of my legacy, a funny story that sums up a flash in time of her childhood. She'll remember I tried and failed sometimes. I worried and loved and did the best I could. We all have these family stories we roll out on holidays or when someone new comes to visit. In my family, it's the time my brother's foot and leg came smashing through my dad's friend's dining room ceiling while the adults sat around the table not knowing the kids had found the crawl space up above. Or the time my mom got hit by a bluefish after my brother and a friend got into a fight after a fishing trip and used their loot for ammunition. Those are the silly things but there are cherished moments there too. I remember my sister holding my older daughter for the first time after my very long, difficult and very scary delivery. She gazed at her full throttle crying and said, "She's going to do something really special with her life." It was an injection of love that held me up then and now.

There are things I hope I am remembered for and things I hope I'm not. After I married my husband, I turned to him one day and said, "There's one thing you need to know." He looked at me, a little unsure. "Make sure the casket is closed," I said. "I don't want anyone seeing me dead." And please, no one can do my hair right. I don't want people remembering me dead with awful hair. Is that terrible of me to think that way? "Put a picture of me on the casket," I've told him. "And make sure it's closed tight." I don't even want HIM looking in there!

Many times during news interviews I've asked someone, "What should we remember about him?" It's not an easy question to answer. There are usually too many things on a list like that. How do you sum up a life? That glow that makes someone who they are? The attraction or the admiration between two people? Sometimes words aren't enough to describe the goodness in someone else.

I know how I hope I will be remembered. I can think of what I want my own personal legacy to be but that's probably not important to you. I think we need to take a look at our own individual wishes and examine the person we are putting out in the world. Think about how others perceive you. Did you ever hear your recorded voice and think, "I sound like that?" We have to listen to who we are, who the world sees us as, and who we want to be. How do we make the people in our lives feel? And is that the fullness of our being? Is there something more?

Ponder those questions for a bit. I'll do the same. One of my favorite things about television news is just connecting with people. You meet all kinds, in every stage of life; in prison, in homeless shelters, in addiction centers, in the office of the CEO. We like to say we're "story tellers" and that's what we are. I love to search and find what's compelling about every person I come across. And there is always, and I mean always, a fascinating story to tell about every single person I meet. I like to find what they would want to be remembered for and celebrate it. Think about how you would tell me your story. What's the lead line of your life? That's your legacy in a sentence.

Kim Howie:

WOW, this is a tough one for me! It's sort of like writing your own eulogy and trying to sum up your life in a paragraph or two. Having said that, I believe that we should all think about the mark we wish to leave on this earth, and then use that as our guiding principle. If I wish for my legacy to include a life lived with kindness, empathy and compassion, I need to navigate life with kindness, empathy and compassion for EVERYONE, not just the select few whom I deem worthy. For me, personally, these qualities are paramount to living my truth and are non-negotiable aspects of meaningful existence.

A few years ago I had my birth chart read by an Astrologist. At the time I knew very little about Astrology, and avoided my horoscope at all costs as I knew my propensity to create self-fulfilling prophecies. After years of traveling on my spiritual journey, I've come to appreciate this propensity as the Law of Attraction or the ability to speak and/or think things into being. Or if you are more science-driven, it's the placebo effect. When we think something is going to impact our lives, those thoughts create the placebo effect. In other words, what we put our attention on expands, and therefore we can literally create our own reality. But back to my birth chart reading. This experience was truly life changing for me. I remember the moment the Astrologist told me that I was going to make an impact on the world. This felt like a blessing and a curse at the same time! I had never thought about my life in terms of its impact on the world, and suddenly I felt this HUGE responsibility to do something impactful! I left there wondering what I could possibly do that would make an impact on the world! Yet I also felt empowered!

I share that experience not to sound important, as I now believe that we are ALL here to make an impact on the world; but rather to explain that our legacy doesn't need to be grand or feel like a heavy responsibility. But rather, it's about living a life filled with meaning, recognizing that we have an impact on each other and on the world. Taking responsibility for our actions and owning our personal power. This is how we create our legacy.

I remember seeing Elizabeth Gilbert, author of Eat, Pray, Love, speak a few years ago, and she talked about how she had been speaking to groups for many years about the importance of finding their passion. Then one day after a talk she received an email from someone who had been in the audience. The person was clearly upset by the talk and expressed how she had been trying for years to uncover her passion, but all of the searching was only leading to frustration. This message had a profound impact on Elizabeth, as she realized that she had been "a passion bully," and was making people who couldn't identify a single passion feel badly about themselves. She went on to explain that there are jackhammers and hummingbirds in the world. Some people simply put their heads down and jackhammer away at their passion; while others like to float around and gently move like a hummingbird from passion to passion in life. I share this story with you as a way of explaining that we don't necessarily need to spend our lives trying to do something special to craft our legacy, but rather recognize that our daily actions add up to a lifetime legacy.

So live your life in the manner in which you want to be remembered. And don't forget to show and tell your loved ones how you feel about them as often as possible. Life is short, and you can never hear the words "I love you" too many times!

Thought-Provoking, Self-Reflection Questions:
1. What is the lead line of your life?
2. What do you want your legacy to be?
3. Are you living your life in alignment with that legacy?

_____

_____

_____

_____

_____

_____

_____

_____

_____

_____

_____

_____

_____

_____

_____

_____

_____

_____

_____

_____

_____

_____

_____

_____

_____

_____

_____

Chapter 16 - Refuel/Health

Laura Gross, MA, LPC
Counselor
Yoga Instructor

"When do you find rewarding time just for you? When do you take a break? Take a vacation? We live in such a high paced society and most of us are operating in a fight or flight type of way and our body reacts to that. It even impacts our emotional status so you have to take a break."

Nancy Werteen:

Frazzled is when you go to the store without even realizing you still have your fuzzy slippers on. I've done that. Frazzled is trying to eat food while brushing your teeth. I've done that. Twice actually. Frazzled is anchoring a whole newscast with a small pink curler in the back of your hair. I've done that too! In my defense, the curler was covered by a layer of hair but still-that's pretty frazzled. I must admit, I'm usually a whirlwind of activity and not very good at the concept of refueling. I'm working on it. There have been moments I've been slammed over head with the realization that I have to slow down. There was the time I literally almost choked to death on a salami sandwich because of trying to eat it while running through the house. I had to use a kitchen bar stool to give myself the Heimlich. That woke me up. Or the time I slipped on some ice while holding my cell phone to my ear with one hand and a bag of groceries in the other, which didn't give me a hand to put down to break my fall. Just got lucky there that I didn't hurt anything major but I had to shake my head at my ridiculousness.

Throughout my life I've had an internal tug of war over the subject of relaxation. That's why I can't do yoga. I'm too impatient. Too naturally hyped up to slow down enough to enjoy it. That and I'm way too tall. It's just too far for me to reach the ground for those downward dog poses. That's another subject, but I'm just fidgety. I literally set competitions for myself for things like grocery shopping. Each week, or twice a week really with as much as I am at the grocery store, I try to see if I can beat my personal best. My record is 28 minutes door to door. Now come on, is this necessary? Of course not, but somehow it seems to make sense at the time. I also come up with those daily "to-do" lists that if I really considered them, I would realize no one could accomplish all that in one day! So this is what I do. I turn household chores into Olympic events and make myself my toughest competitor.

When you live this way, you wake up one day and realize you're usually out of breath, all day, every day. You realize taking a great deep breath feels like a cold glass of water in the desert. You realize enough is enough. At least that's what has happened to me. I guess part of the resistance has been that nasty perfection problem that pokes its nose in most things. How can I stop? How can I slow down? There's too much to do and too many people to beat me doing it. But I'm learning that's no way to live. I'm learning that being out of breath makes me feel like I've just stepped off a curb and looked up to see a car heading right for me. It makes me feel exhausted. It makes me feel like a failure. I'm learning to just stop. To breathe. Deeply. I'm learning to figure out what I enjoy and then revel in it. Even if it's just 20 minutes to read a book or stare out the window or even pick my nose. Whatever it is that allows me to check out and take in some oxygen.

But there's more to it than that, isn't there? It's not enough to just breathe sometimes, in life you have to really inhale. How many of us make enough time to just be with our girlfriends? We did when we were younger right? We'd waste away a whole afternoon just talking and giggling and having tea or wine or whatever. Who does that anymore? There are kids to worry about and husbands and jobs. When things were really hectic when my girls were little, I used to stop sometimes and lie on the grass with them and look at the clouds. We'd imagine unicorns and horses and a fairy princess or two. Wow, did that take me away. Some of my most cherished memories are wrapped up in that simple activity. I can smell the grass and feel the warmth of the sun on my face, a small hand in mine, our synchronized breathing. Doesn't get much better than that.

My goal these days, and I'm promising myself I won't make it a competition, is to find those clouds again. I see a friend from college every year in December in New York City for lunch. We sit down and start babbling like we were just together yesterday. We talk about our spouses and kids and television and aspirations and of course, we reminisce. We remember this time and that time and laugh our asses off. And when I leave, I think, "Why don't I do that more often?" I think it's about giving yourself permission, letting yourself off the hook for a little while. Sometimes it's just about a giggle and a smile and an old friend. That's refueling for sure, but I think refueling is a bit more complex.

Day to day, I have to say tennis is the refuel for me. While that, of course, is a competition, it's also a way to just check out. You really can't think about anything but that small green ball and where it is and whether it's heading for your face. If you do, you're likely to get pummeled. Everything else kind of falls away. The intensity relaxes me as insane as that sounds. I guess that has to do with exercise. If I don't play tennis, I like to walk. My husband and I will do a good 4 miles. We talk about anything or nothing. It's the one time there are no phones, no kids, no television, just us. Now, he is as competitive as I am, so we also find ways to see who can go the fastest or the farthest, but the goal is to move and move as much as we can. I've found that if I go two days without exercise, I'm basically a bitch on wheels, so I really don't mess with the exercise regimen. I tell people I have a "business meeting," code for tennis match, or "important assignment," code for walking date. I do what I have to do to make sure what I need is built into my schedule so I don't even have to think about it.

I've had times where my body and my soul were starving for food, for fuel to inject energy and joy into my life but not anymore. It just feels too good to put some of that magic back inside and help it grow. I'm still worried about wasting time, but I think that's okay, as long as I remember that wasting time is subjective and your definition might be different from mine. I may need to remind myself that putting time back into me and how I feel and think could never be a waste. And if the "to-do" list doesn't get "to-done" today, is that really such a big deal? It'll be there tomorrow, just as looming I'm sure.

Kim Howie:

As a Health Coach, this topic is near and dear to my heart! My passion lies in helping others be proactive and take control of their health before it becomes an issue that requires their reactive attention.

I remember facilitating a training course many years ago (long before my health coaching days) when I worked in Human Resources for a large corporation in the financial services industry, where I walked participants through a process of identifying their top five values in life. What struck me as interesting was that health came up as the number one value for so many participants. They would express to me that none of the other values would matter as much if they didn't have their health. As a healthy young person, I hadn't yet realized the value of health and its impact on all other aspects of life.

Fast forward 20 years to my own personal hormonal health crisis, and it suddenly became crystal clear what they meant. It was at that moment that I recognized how my health impacted every aspect of my life. When my hormones went haywire, I literally thought I was going crazy! I felt as though I was having an out of body experience. I'd see myself yelling at my children and wonder "why am I yelling? I'm not a yeller! Why can't I seem to control my emotions?" I knew I was "off", but I had no idea why or how to fix it. After a few months of riding the emotional rollercoaster, gaining 20 pounds, and wondering why my period stopped (after taking several pregnancy tests that came back negative), I finally went to the gynecologist and begged him to give me a pill to fix it. Much to my dismay, he began to talk to me about my diet. He told me to go home, eliminate all packaged food and eat only real, whole foods for one month, and then come back to see him. He said if I was still struggling he would write me a prescription.

I left his office feeling a combination of confused and furious. I didn't have the slightest idea what food had to do with my hormones, and how dare he tell me that my diet was responsible for my health issues! I thought I ate healthy. I was choosing low calorie foods and even using no-calorie spray butter on my vegetables! But out of respect for my doctor, a bit of desperation, and my desire to prove my doctor wrong (as in my mind I truly believed that I'd be back in his office in one month getting my prescription), I gave this whole foods diet a try.

Much to my surprise, within one week of changing my diet, my moods began to balance and the weight began to melt off. By the end of the month, my period came back, my emotions normalized and all of the weight I had gained was gone. I was astonished! I just had to learn more about the connection between the foods we eat and our physical and emotional health. I decided to enroll in the Institute for Integrative Nutrition. During the course of my studies I learned over 100 different dietary theories, but what resonated with me the most was the holistic approach to health, and recognizing that living a healthy life involves more than just eating healthy foods!

In my book, *The Simple Recipe For A Healthy, Balanced Life*, I talk about the ingredients necessary to be proactive with your health. These include a whole foods diet, exercise, sleep, stress reduction, self-care, healthy relationships and a positive mindset focused on happiness, joy, and purpose. This is the foundation of how I coach my clients; however, I have come to recognize that mindset is at the root of all of these ingredients. If our attitude about getting healthy feels like deprivation rather than joy, our efforts to gain and maintain a healthy lifestyle will be futile.

One of my favorite sayings is that health is not the absence of disease, but rather the presence of vitality. Getting healthy for the sake of avoiding disease can be effective; however, I find that having a deeper

WHY helps me to stay committed to my healthy lifestyle! My why is that I want to feel good physically and emotionally, and I know from personal experience that when I am not following my wellness plan, I do NOT feel good - neither physically nor emotionally! And what matters even more to me is that I know that when I put crap in my body, I feel like crap and I tend to treat myself and others like crap!

My wellness plan includes fueling my body with healthy foods as well as taking time out to refuel. I know that stress reduction and self-care play an important role in our overall health and wellbeing. Personally, this has always meant scheduling "me time" into my day. That time always includes exercise and meditation, because for me, that's like brushing my teeth, if I don't do it, I feel terrible! But I also try at least once a month to include something special like a nail appointment, a massage, a lunch date with a friend, shopping, or simply a few minutes of quiet time to read, relax or take a bubble bath. This time helps to re-energize me and keep me centered so that I can be proactive and make healthy choices that serve me, rather than reactive which oftentimes leads me to choices that deplete me and create a vicious cycle that continues to steal my joy. If you don't already make time to refuel, I strongly urge you to do so. You'll be pleasantly surprised by the impact it has on your physical and emotional health.

Thought-Provoking, Self-Reflection Questions:
1. What do you do to refuel?
2. Is health a priority in your life?
3. What change can you make right now that will impact your overall health and wellbeing?

_____

_____

_____

_____

_____

_____

_____

_____

_____

_____

_____

_____

_____

_____

_____

_____

_____

_____

_____

_____

Chapter 17 - Self Care

Paula Di Marco Young
Registered Nurse, Marketing Director for Young Medical Spa® - Center Valley & Lansdale, PA

"It's a shame I have to stop and think about how pretty a flower is, or a sunset. It's a shame I have to do that because my mind just isn't there because I'm always thinking, 'what do you have to do for the kids, or work, or somebody else' and I just never stop. I never stop."

Nancy Werteen:

I think part of caring for yourself is figuring out who the heck you really are. It's seeing yourself for all your weaknesses and faults and saying, "I like you anyway and I need to take care of you." But that's a wild ride isn't it? It takes a lot of work I think to get to that place. When I look back at my late teens, early 20s, I realize my goal then was to be a person who pleased other people. I am ashamed to think about the ways I tried to reinvent myself because it was what I thought someone else wanted. I remember vividly applying for one of my first jobs and I said, "I'm here to interview for the position." The manager of the department actually said, "Missionary or doggie style?" I was so naive and so unsure of myself I didn't say a word. I just stood there-mute. What an asshole!! Him, not me! What I would love to have said to that jerk. But I didn't. The crass thing to say is that I didn't have the balls but he sure did! The truth is I just didn't know myself, didn't have much confidence and didn't think I could stand up for myself with conviction. I learned as experiences unfolded and hard knocks came knocking to find my voice.

I remember one of the first times I went out on a date with my now husband. Coming off an 8-year relationship, I had clarity about what I did and didn't want for sure. In my late 20s by this time, when he took me to a gathering and decided to hang out with the guys upstairs and leave me with a group of women I didn't know, I got him out to the car and told him, "You want to go out with me, you go out with me. You want to go out with the guys, go out with the guys. But you can't have it both ways." I surprised even myself at the time, but he loved it. He liked that I stood up for myself. I had learned a lot by that point about making myself clear and avoiding misunderstandings.

Of course, as time has gone on I've improved on it as most of us do as we age. In my 30s, I didn't think twice about standing up for my kids, questioning difficult people, challenging decisions. You hit 40 and you think, "I've been dealing with this crap or that crap for 25 years and I am done with it." And please, by 50, you're having so many hot flashes, you have no tolerance for anything even slightly irritating. But then there's also an epiphany. At least there was for me. And maybe we all get to it in our own time. For me, there's been a realization that when I look inward, I have to take care of that little girl who's in there-the one I sort of forgot about. She's silly and kind and scared. She gets her feelings hurt and wonders if she's done the right thing or made the right decision. She tries her best and wants to be loved. That's who I need to care for. That's who I need to cherish.

For a long time, I didn't want to see her. I wanted to pretend she doesn't exist. That works for a while until it suddenly doesn't work anymore. What works is finding out who she is and what makes her happy and then doing it. It's uncovering the layers of protection and exposing the scabs to the air. And I think when you do that, you shore up the very foundation of who you are. So when the storms come, you don't fall apart.

Taking care of myself these days means learning to love the whole package and letting the people who love me unwrap that package too. It takes trust and guts and vulnerability but it's what makes you feel alive and truly loved. It's what makes you feel complete and protected. For me, looking in makes me understand I need to be valued and there are certain things I demand I get or don't get. I have to be honest with myself to clearly see how to care for my whole self and I have to let other people know the secret too.

Recently, after a confusing situation with my husband when I was feeling especially vulnerable, I just said, "I'm feeling really scared. I need you to tell me if you're pissed and if you're not, then I need you to tell me that too and let me off the hook." Of course I came barreling down the stairs some 30 minutes after this alleged encounter took place that he had already forgotten about. I rounded the corner of the family room while he sat on the couch with Cheez-It® crumbs on his sweatshirt watching football on TV and blurted out this heartfelt truth that seemed so heavy to me. He looked up confused and said, "Of course I'm not mad. I love you." That simple. It's amazing what happens when I am honest with myself and others.

Self-care has a different meaning for all of us I think. You just have to find out who your own self is and how to care for her in the best way you can.

Kim Howie:

Many of us spend the majority of our day pleasing and caring for others at home, in the office, or out in the community. This may ultimately lead to feelings of resentment, particularly if our needs always come last.

Overstressed and overworked, we often find ourselves hitting the point where we feel emotionally bankrupt, especially when we lack outlets or resources for managing our multiple responsibilities and the never-ending "to do" lists. If we continually give to others, we will feel depleted and will wake up one day to realize that our well has run dry and we have no more to give. Just as we need to refill our car's gas tank, it's imperative that we refill our own personal well.

We must first take care of ourselves, so that we can then take care of others. Think about the airplane analogy where parents are instructed to place the oxygen mask on themselves before they place it on their child. When we nourish ourselves, those around us reap the rewards. As we decide to take care of ourselves in a more attentive, proactive, and nurturing way, we are protecting and replenishing our energy reserves so that we actually have more to offer our loved ones and the outside world.

The physical benefits from practicing self-care are numerous. They span from relaxation and stress reduction to disease prevention. Many of these benefits stem from lower cortisol levels. When our body is in a state of relaxation it does not produce cortisol (the stress hormone), therefore decreasing the risk of heart disease and dementia, while improving immune system function and decreasing symptoms from autoimmune diseases.

Self-care can also improve our emotional health. Many forms of self-care help to increase the production of our happy hormones. Having a well-cared-for body can help us to feel good about ourselves and our lives. In addition, taking time to care for ourselves can convey to others that we value ourselves and remind them that our needs are important too. In many ways, we teach others how to treat us by demonstrating that we find ourselves worthy of care. Studies show that long-term feelings of well-being are often associated with those who actively make time for their own self-care, pursuits, and interests.

Self-care can also make us better caregivers. Research shows that people who spend their time only caring for others are at a higher risk for becoming burned out. And those who neglect their own needs and forget to nurture themselves typically experience deeper levels of unhappiness, low self-esteem, and more feelings of resentment than those who reserve time to recharge their batteries.

For me, self-care includes eating healthy foods, exercising regularly, getting ample sleep, practicing stress reduction and mindfulness every day.

Some additional suggestions for self-care include:

- Meditation or prayer
- Yoga, tai chi, or chi gong
- Taking a walk in nature
- Taking a "news fast"
- Listening to soothing music
- Journaling
- Spending quality time with loved ones
- Enjoying creative outlets

When selecting your form of self-care, Cheryl Richardson, author of *The Art of Extreme Self Care*, states that it's a good idea to discover when, where, why and how you feel deprived, as this will help guide you on how best to approach your self-care. She says asking yourself questions like "what do I need more of or less of right now?" or "who or what is causing me to feel resentful and why?" will provide insight into the type of self-care you need. She also recommends creating an absolute NO list. This list serves as a reminder of the things we refuse to tolerate in our lives, as well as a reminder that it's okay to say no. We often find ourselves spread too thin because we are afraid to say no. We need to create boundaries around our time as well as learn to ask for and accept help from others when needed.

Regardless of what activity you choose, be sure to put yourself back on your priority list, and create a routine that includes time for self-care.

Thought-Provoking, Self-Reflection Questions:
1. What do you currently do for self-care?
2. What can you add to your routine to help fill up your well?
3. What's on your absolute no list?

_____

_____

_____

_____

_____

_____

_____

_____

_____

_____

_____

_____

_____

_____

_____

_____

_____

_____

_____

_____

_____

_____

_____

_____

_____

Chapter 18 – Friendship

Joellen Reichenbach
Daughter, sister, wife, friend, entrepreneur
Owner of Select Sales, Creative Marketing Solutions

"Our goal is truly to love one another, be there for each other, but then our roles and responsibilities impact that. So I get challenged with saying 'Did I create a memory today that will be remembered tomorrow?' because I'm not guaranteed tomorrow."

Nancy Werteen:

It finally happened. My pre-teen informed me, very sweetly and apologetically, that she'd actually rather be with her girlfriends than with me. Well, how could that be? Oddly enough, I get it. I understand where she's coming from and I remember feeling that way, that my girlfriends were more important than anything else. And thankfully, I've been lucky enough to have a few who have been there with me in every crisis and triumph as the years have passed. And what a treat that's been.

I remember when I met one of my lifelong girlfriends. Let me take you there. It's 1982. The year John Belushi died. We don't have cell phones or pagers or even computers. We don't even have debit cards. On Friday afternoon, we have to estimate how much money we might need for the weekend and then go to the bank and get it. I am 19.

Standing in a corner of a crowded kitchen with too much noise and too many faces I don't know listening to a scratchy Pat Benatar album on someone's stereo, I'm feeling like the queen of the dorks despite the gel in my hair and my blue eyeshadow. There with my then boyfriend, the first person he introduces me to blurts out, "You didn't tell me she was so TALL." Course this is followed up with a litany of comments like, "Can you believe how tall she is?" and "Do you guys even line up?" Now there's laughter and it's like I'm not even there. I'm handed a beer and the party takes its official run out of the starting gate.

By the time the stereo gets to Let it Whip by The Dazz Band, the boyfriend is in the other room and I'm awkwardly drumming my fingers on my cup of beer. Just then a woman blazes into the kitchen in the highest heels I've ever seen. Even with the boost, she barely clears five feet. She smiles at me and says, "Hey there" and then "Great top." Now my top was hideous I remember. Faux leather. Cheetah pattern. But it was the 80s and that explains that. So we start talking in that way you do with someone you instantly connect with. We're chatting and chatting and suddenly I don't feel like the awkward tall girl, I feel great! After a time, the then boyfriend sweeps back in the kitchen. "Oh you met Nancy," he says. "Yes," she answers. "You didn't tell me she was so beautiful." And the rest is history.

Since then, we've been through three husbands, three kids and three states. With our busy lives, it can be years before we see each other face to face. But whenever we do, it's like we were together just yesterday even though yesterday was a long time ago. What a gift to have a friend like that-someone who truly applauds when something good happens to you and whose heart aches when something goes horribly wrong.

Throughout our lives, we make all kinds of friends. Friends at work, friends because our husbands know each other, friends because our kids play together. When my youngest daughter was around 2-years-old, I met another mom in the neighborhood who also had a 2-year-old and was also 40 when she had him. We bonded instantly and found two other moms nearby with kids the same age and proceeded to have weekly playdates that usually involved a ton of Play-Doh® being smashed into someone's carpet. But in those years, she became another lifeline for me. We used to call each other in the afternoons that seemed to take days with fussy toddlers underfoot. We'd each slide out of earshot-she in her pantry and me in my garage-and we'd let loose the worst curses we could think of. "The f*$@king laundry!" "B#%& S@* on that." And on and on we'd go. Eventually, we'd be laughing and feeling much calmer and ready for the next crisis that would surely come our way.

I have another dear friend whose life seems destined to parallel mine. Our children, our beliefs and values, our personalities seem to glue us together with an unstoppable grip. I remember one of the first times I had a conversation with her beyond the smile and polite nod that came from having two girls in the same school. She was on the other side of some swine flu type ridiculousness that swept through her family and kept her housebound for two weeks. We bumped into each other in the parking lot of Wal-Mart® and blabbed and blabbed. She, probably just starving for human contact, and I, happy to make a new friend. From the start, I loved her humor and her attitude and since then, the blabbing hasn't stopped. But it's more than that. When I fractured my back, she was the first one to sweep in with lasagna in hand and as I recall, enough food for a small army.

When you think of it, friendship is a lot like being in love. You meet someone and you can't wait to see her again. You want to find out everything about her, hear her stories, her opinions. You think of her when she's not with you. You get closer and closer and then you find yourself asking her for advice and turning to her for a dose of strength and cheerleading when you need it. Her stability helps to steer your ship.

As an adult, my most constant female friend has been my sister. Now, like most siblings, we were not two peas in a pod growing up. As I can recall, I irritated the hell out of her. And truly, I deserved her wrath. As the younger sister, I always thought she was way cooler than me. How could I resist not trying to be like her? This drove her crazy, especially since this effort usually involved me stealing her clothes for a little day out of the closet. She's three-and-a-half years older than me and basically has gone through everything before me: marriage, childbirth, menopause. We both have two children who are both seven years apart. She's been my guide, my confidant, my calm. I can't imagine how many times I've asked, "How did you handle/feel/manage this or that?" She's always there for me with advice, support and a kind word.

It's that support that puts our friendships on such a pedestal, don't you think? Being there for each other and needing each other with a desperation that's as vital as it is terrifying at times. And just when you think you know all there is to know about friendships, life throws a curveball. At least it did for me. My curveball is Kim. I join a tennis club and find this person so amazing and fascinating with this outlook that rubs off on everyone she touches like the cool water of a sprinkler on a hot summer day.

She's taught me that there are some friends who put out a welcome mat and let you know that it's okay to show up with your hair a mess and your shoes untied. She'll invite you in with her arms open wide. She's taught me that one person's positive attitude can literally change the world. She's taught me that life is too precious to sit with small talk instead of taking the opportunity to really connect with someone else. She's proven to me that she'll hold the most fragile part of me with all her heart.

The seasons of my life have been defined by the female friends who laughed with me, who held me up, who allowed me to embrace them and who accepted my love with a full heart. So yeah, I'll let my daughter off the hook on this one and let her hang out with her friends instead of me.

Kim Howie:

I love the quote "Life is a journey we are not meant to take alone." I can't imagine living life without good friends! I have always enjoyed the company of others, and the energy they bring into my life.

Harvard recently published a 74-year study that identified the number one factor contributing to our health is the quality of our relationships. I didn't find this to be surprising, as I believe that human connection is a vital part of living a joy-filled life. But not just any human connection, it needs to be authentic and life-enhancing. Sometimes we have relationships that are not life enhancing, and sometimes they are downright detrimental. It's so important that we practice discernment and recognize the difference.

Dr. Brene Brown talks about finding your balcony friends in her book *Daring Greatly*. She explains that these are the people who come to cheer you on in life. She differentiates between these people and the ones who "sit in the cheap seats"; the ones who will walk away or stab you in the back when you fall. The key is knowing the difference.

This was a bit of a problem for me early on in life, as I've always been a people pleaser who wanted to be liked by everyone. When I look back now, I can see that I was somewhat of a chameleon, changing who I was in order to fit in everywhere I went. This was my way of trying to avoid being excluded. I thought that the more friends you had the better. You see, I never liked to be alone, as I hated to feel lonely. However, I've come to realize that you can be alone without feeling lonely, just as you can be surrounded by others and feel extremely lonely. Discernment makes all the difference. This realization came after doing many years of inner work to figure out who I really am, what's important for me, and learning to stay true to my authentic self.

When I decided to prioritize joy in my life, I made a shift in my thinking from "why don't they like me" to "does their energy make me feel joyful or depleted?" Using this as a barometer, I started spending more time with people who enhanced my energy and less time with those who depleted it. This was not a judgment about the person, but rather an observation about how I felt when I was in their presence.

I found that this process of discernment enabled me to create more meaningful friendships in my life. I also recognize my responsibility to enhance the lives of those whom I am fortunate enough to call my friends. I realize that friendship is a two-way street, and I need to hold myself accountable for being the kind of friend that I desire to have in life. Sometimes we get so focused on having our own needs met that we don't take the time to look closely to determine whether we are giving as much as we are getting.

I like to use the platinum rule rather than the golden rule. This says to treat others as THEY wish to be treated rather than as YOU wish to be treated. I need to remember that we are all unique, and just because I like to be open and share my feelings with others doesn't mean that I should expect the same in return. This has been a difficult lesson for me to learn, and one that I am still learning! Ultimately, I believe that we are more alike than we are different, but we are all individuals with our own personalities and our own life experiences that have shaped who we are and how we show up in the world. Learning to respect and appreciate those differences in others is an important part of creating genuine, loving friendships.

Nancy and I laugh when we talk about how different we are, and our fundamental approaches to life. We sum it up in the statement that Nancy likes to button things up and I like to let them unfold. We play tennis together and she is way more aggressive than I am at the net and much more competitive on the court. Yet, our differences actually make us the perfect partners on and off the court. We balance and stretch each other in wonderful ways. Our friendship is based on loving respect for each other's differences, and we always check in with one another when we think we may have stepped over the line and said or done something that may have upset the other. To me, this is the key to genuine friendship! We need to fact check the stories we make up in our head, ensure that we treasure our similarities AND our differences, and always give the other person the benefit of the doubt!

I like to live by the quote that people come into our lives for a reason, a season or a lifetime. Some friends are meant to accompany us on a lifelong journey, while others may be there to help us through a particular season or to guide us to learn a specific lesson in life. Each and every one is meaningful and priceless.

Friendship is a gift to be treasured and never taken for granted. I have been blessed with many wonderful friends throughout my life, and they have all enhanced this amazing journey!

Thought-Provoking, Self-Reflection Questions:
1. Do you practice discernment in your life?
2. Who are your balcony friends?
3. When is the last time you told them how much they mean to you?

_____

_____

_____

_____

_____

_____

_____

_____

_____

_____

_____

_____

_____

_____

_____

_____

_____

_____

_____

_____

_____

_____

_____

_____

_____

_____

Chapter 19 - What Would You Tell Your Younger Self?

Kassie Hilgert
President and CEO of Artsquest

"If you're too focused you can miss what's happening in the moment in the day and so often those smaller moments have the lessons and so to me it would be slow down, you're going to get there. You're going to get the experience. It's all going to come to you if you keep trying but just relax a little."

Nancy Werteen:

Like most families, we love watching videos from years ago. My girls were so little and good grief, was I ever that young? We laugh at how cute they were and how ridiculous some of my outfits looked. The last time we did this, as I watched, I remembered not just the smiling faces, but the stress and worries of some of those times. I saw myself pronouncing, "butt-er-fly" in very exaggerated tones to my then 2-year-old and I remembered. I remembered being so worried because she was a late talker. Would she speak normally? Would she be okay? Did I do something to cause her tardiness? There I was in another clip to my then 11-year-old, "You're perfect just the way you are." Would she ever find the confidence in herself that she so deserved? Time after time, I could see my worries. I thought, if only we had a crystal ball during difficult times. We could see how things turn out and then stop worrying so much. Hmmm. I spent a lot of time on the worry wheel I tell you and for what? That certainly didn't change the outcome of anything. So listen up younger self. Chill out. Seriously. Stop worrying so much.

We all tend to do this, don't we? We worry our way from one stage of our lives to the next. We want everything to turn out just right. But what is "just right" anyway? Certainly your just right is different from mine. If only we could embrace where we are when we're there.

Let me tell you what Kim does. Throughout our Wisdom Coalition journey, whenever we have a setback, she says something like, "It's unfolding perfectly. It's exactly the way it should be." "Alright, alright," I usually grumble. But lately, I'm realizing Kim is totally on to something. So, I've been trying it-even with little things. I get in the car and realize I have to get gas and it's freezing and I have no gloves and will be late, I stop and think, "It's alright, it's unfolding exactly as it should be." And then I feel better. I'm not so worried. I'm not so stressed. And the big things-wow does it work there! Right now I'm all in a lather about my college daughter's future and helping her decide to go to medical school or not. You know what I told her? It's all unfolding perfectly. It's exactly as it should be. Sigh…what a relief and I was worried!!!

My second lesson for my younger self is to trust that you'll find your path. I remember struggling so intently with decisions because what if I made the wrong choice about this or that? About 8 weeks before I was going to get married, totally out of the blue, I get this job offer in another state literally tripling my salary. I wring my hands. I curse. I cry. I can't figure it out. What's the "right" decision I wonder? Once I made the decision to stay where I was, I thought, "What the heck was I doubting myself for?" I didn't want to go anywhere. I was crazy in love and that's all I could think about. But I had to serve myself a big helping of angst just because that's what I did in those days.

In her book, *Feel the Fear and Do it Anyway*, Susan Jeffers talks a lot about how fear is really at the root of many of our decisions. She says we create an image for what we want out of a decision but then once we make that decision, we need to throw that picture away or risk becoming chained to an idea and missing the opportunities right in front of us. She says we have to tell ourselves that "whatever happens as a result of your decision, you'll handle it!" I love that. So there's no right or wrong, there's just a decision. Just a choice to go one way or the other. I'd tell myself, embrace your choices, don't look back and plunge forward all the time!

I'd also tell myself to get to know someone called you a little better. My younger self kind of threw darts at a dartboard to see which ones would stick at times instead of taking aim at the center I wanted to be connected with. I'd say show up and be fully present in every moment, relationship and even every challenge. And as part of that, I'd say realize that you can't control or take responsibility for anyone's actions or feelings except your own. Now let me explain that because it isn't as narcissistic as it sounds. For a long time, I focused on trying to make sure everyone else was happy. And I have to admit, I'm still struggling with this one. Anytime my husband walks in the door in a grouchy mood, the first words out of my mouth are, "Are you mad at me?" Why jump all the way there? I've spent my whole life struggling to let go of trying to manage everyone else's happiness. Of course, that's completely impossible to do! Now I see my older daughter wrestling with the same thing. Even when she was a toddler, I'd say, "DON'T TOUCH THE STOVE." She'd nod her head and never move toward that stove again. My little daughter as a toddler, on the other hand, when I said, "don't touch the stove," she'd accidently "fall" into the stove area, do a dance that included a pirouette into the stove, or sneak a little touch behind my back. Funny how different kids are! Unfortunately for her, my older one, she's inherited my people pleaser gene, but I've been pointing out to her the futility of these efforts and seriously trying to practice what I preach.

And this last piece of advice, I can't help myself. I'd say stop criticizing that body!! Let me give you a little newsflash of what it turns into-of what dents and what flops in about 35 years. Savor it. I'd say stop the negative talk. It's ridiculous. You're fabulous. Why do we do that to ourselves? Waste time putting ourselves down. Over the years, I've heard my daughters and their friends sometimes lamenting that they "aren't pretty" or "don't look good enough" for this or that. It's heartbreaking.

The other day I heard this definition of Hell. That it's when we die and meet the person we could have become. Let that sink in a minute. I'd tell myself, free yourself to become who you are meant to be without fear or criticism. Charge ahead with zest and confidence and the faith that every step you take leads you where you should be. That and enjoy the ride.

Kim Howie:

I would tell my younger self to listen to your gut and always be true to who you are, not allowing others' opinions to sway you or make you doubt yourself. Recognize that people are all entitled to their opinions, and there's nothing wrong with being open to what they have to say, but no one's opinion of you or anything else is more valuable than your own.

The reason I would tell my younger self this is because I placed way too much emphasis on what other people thought about me and their advice for what was best for me. It wasn't until much later in life that I realized that people mean well, but they don't know better than I do what's best for me!

Along those same lines, I would tell my younger self that if you aim to please everyone, you will end up pleasing no one (including yourself)! As a people pleaser, I can't count the number of times that I worked so hard to make everyone happy only to realize that all of that effort was wasted because I actually made things worse rather than better, and in the end, I was miserable!

I'd be sure to tell my younger self to live in the present moment. I wasted so much time beating myself up about the past or worrying about the future. Realizing now that the present moment is where the joy is taking place at all times.

I would also tell my younger self that expectations are disappointments waiting to happen. When we set expectations for life, especially ones that are dependent on the actions of others, we are setting ourselves up to be let down. I've learned over the years to let life unfold without being attached to a specific outcome. This is extremely helpful during times of stress. Letting go of the need to control the outcome or someone else's actions takes so much stress out of life.

And finally I'd tell my younger self to have faith that life truly is unfolding perfectly at all times!

Thought-Provoking, Self-Reflection Questions:
1. What would you tell your younger self?
2. How are you applying that knowledge to your life now?
3. With whom can you share that advice now?

_____

_____

_____

_____

_____

_____

_____

_____

_____

_____

_____

_____

_____

_____

_____

_____

_____

_____

_____

_____

_____

_____

_____

_____

Chapter 20 - What I Know For Sure

Dr. Nichola Gutgold
Professor – Author – Speaker

"Staying true to your nature is key to happiness and self-actualization."

Nancy Werteen:

I have a close family member who is an alcoholic. Not the kind who drinks too much at a party and puts a lampshade on his head. No, he's the kind who disappears for weeks or even months and resurfaces to break our hearts again and again. We've spent the better of 40 years trying to save him from himself, but we just can't seem to do it. At this point, it's like he's drowning in the rapids of a wild river. We're standing on the banks and we can see him out there going slowly under. There have been times in the past when he's reached for a lifeline-a log or a tree to grasp on to to try to save himself-but he doesn't anymore. He just sinks. We have stood on the banks of that river for ages. We've even jumped in at times but soon found that you can't save someone who doesn't want to be saved unless you want to drown right along with him. We've pleaded, we've cried, we've yelled, tried everything to convince him to pull himself out. We've reached out our hands. At times he's grabbed for them. Not anymore. And now we're faced with an awful choice; stand there and watch or turn away. It's an absolute heartbreak.

Because of this, what I know for sure, and forgive me if this isn't profound, what I know for sure is that you can't piss your life away. You have a responsibility to yourself and the people who love you to make the most of everything you've got. You have to literally count your blessings. Every single one.

The more people we meet and the farther we travel down this path of discovery that is The Wisdom Coalition, the more I feel a sense of urgency. I see people wasting so much time on complaints and complacency. I know for sure we can cultivate the life we want. Our lives are ripe for building, for developing, for thriving.

For a long time, I lived my life putting one foot in front of the other. Sometimes I'd make a mental assessment. Was it a good day? Was I happy? Well that depends on what's going on right? Depends on how people are treating me. Depends on what's happening in my life-what's going right and what isn't. But that's just totally off base. What I've discovered is that I can chose joy any time I want! Doesn't make a hill of beans what my circumstances are.

When a child is born, no mother or father says, "I hope she's mediocre. I hope she doesn't live up to her potential. I hope she doesn't make the most of what she's been given." That's silly. Of course no parent would say that. But why do we settle for these qualities sometimes in ourselves? I know for sure that the tremendous gift of our life is that we can make it the best it can be! I know for sure that small efforts dole out big payoffs. I know for sure that we can fulfill all the dreams we have for ourselves.

I know for sure that we'll regret not loving with a whole heart. We'll regret settling for laziness and cutting corners. I know for sure that we all have the tools within us to improve our futures no matter our challenges or circumstances.

And here's the worst thing. I know for sure how horrific it is for a life to disintegrate. It's awful for the person and for everyone around him.

For sure I know that this joy journey we speak of is vital and the clock is ticking. Every night we go to sleep is one day less to share with those who bring us peace and love. Every day that goes by moves the big hand closer to the end. There's no more time to be wishy washy, to wait for someone else to bring you joy or to hope that joy will come to you eventually.

The time is now. For discovery. For fulfillment. For joy.

Kim Howie:

What I know for sure is that our life is always moving towards what we are thinking about. Our thoughts are the foundation for our actions, and what we choose to focus on in life colors our reality. There are certainly plenty of negative things going on in the world and in our everyday experiences, but focusing on them only magnifies them and certainly doesn't make them any better. Choosing to focus on the positive aspects in life creates a brighter existence and promotes an attitude of joy. And why would anyone choose to live without joy?

What I also know for sure is that our expectations shape our experiences. Basically, what we look for in life is what we will see. So if we make a choice to look for things that bring us joy, we will find more joy in life. Neuroscience and Positive Psychology have proven that we can actually train our brains to be more optimistic; it's called learned optimism, and it has a measurable impact on our overall health and wellbeing.

And what I know for sure, FOR SURE, is that we are all more alike than we are different. This is the foundation of shared humanity. We all have the same basic needs and desires in life. We all want to be loved and appreciated for who we are just the way we are. We all want to be seen, heard, and understood. And we all desire to live a life filled with love and joy.

Why then do we spend so much of our time focusing on things that deplete us of love and joy? Why do we judge others for being their unique selves when we want to be appreciated for being our unique selves? Why do we go through life fighting to be heard, but not taking the time to really listen to what others are saying?

What I know for sure is that life would be so much easier if we could all stop and really recognize that we are all in this together, longing for the same end result ~ a joy-filled, respectful, love-filled world! That's the power of a pivot! Stop hard and pivot towards joy, recognizing your personal power to create your own reality!

Thought-Provoking, Self-Reflection Questions:
1. What do you know for sure?
2. Who would benefit from your advice?
3. How can you share that advice with others?

_____

_____

_____

_____

_____

_____

_____

_____

_____

_____

_____

_____

_____

_____

_____

_____

_____

_____

_____

_____

_____

_____

_____

_____

_____

Chapter 21 - Vulnerability

Karen Finocchio
One Tough Muther Podcast Host
Founder/OTM Army
Mother of four, grandmother

> *"In our weakest moments, we become the strongest. Failure is an incident, not a tattoo. What you're telling yourself is what you process so tell yourself positive things. Be positive with yourself, it makes a huge difference."*

Nancy Werteen:

Want to laugh? When Kim and I started The Wisdom Coalition, I went on this big rant that I revisited often about how I was not "going to talk about my feelings" damn it. Not to her or anyone else. Have you read the last 20 chapters? It's pretty much me with my metaphoric mental pants pulled down. I still can't believe what's come out of my keyboard. What the hell happened? Oddly, I seem to have no control over what I write here. Many times I'd think about the title of one of the chapters, go to sleep and wake up at 4:00am with words circulating in my head. I'd get up, bang them out on the computer, go back to bed and then be pretty surprised by what I read in the morning.

All of this has me perplexed but here's what I am thinking. This process of looking inside and pulling out the cobwebs, dusting them off and peering around the rooms is refreshing. I remember when my older daughter was about 5 years old she came to us one day and said, "I finally realized I'm not a cartoon character." We still laugh about it but what she was saying, I think, is that she had been discovering herself.

She pondered and wondered who she is, how and why. We all do this, unwrap that secret box that has the recipe for us. But then we get scared and tuck it neatly away once again-unsure of who should see it-unsure who to trust it with.

There have been mornings I've read what I wrote and thought-holy cow-DELETE-quick. And to be honest, delete I have. But this process of considering what things like love and regret mean to me, has been cathartic. I admit to waking up some mornings and before hitting the delete, doing a little mental dry heaving after reading what I saw on the screen. I had no idea what all was in there. So I urge you to do the same-not the dry heaving part-but the self-examination part. Seems to me we have to really know our true selves in order to show up fully in our lives and our relationships. For me, the clothes in that washing machine inside my head needed to come out and sit in the sun for a while because they were getting really moldy.

When you think about your life, your past, your experiences, your hopes, it's a personal process. But I think putting those things under a microscope allows you to find the cancer waiting to metastasize. And if you can look and be honest and find the vulnerability you have, you can decide what to do with that. You can decide to be honest about it and offer it to other people you hope will treat it and you with love and kindness. Doesn't that scare the hell out of you? It does me. But I think the alternative is worse. It's worse to worry so much about showing the part of you that's really the open scab that you can never ever let it heal.

What's more, I think the people we love want the honor of being trusted with what we find makes us weak, messy and not at all perfect. This exchange, this give and take of acceptance and love for who you REALLY are, is the only way you can give love back. The God's honest truth is we are all vulnerable and weak in certain areas whether we want to admit it or not! And at the end of the day I think we all want the same things: love, acceptance, joy and then some.

I have found my vulnerability is a tug of war between who I really am, who I think I SHOULD be and who I really want to be. It all gets mixed up sometimes so that I can't think straight. Ask me a question and I don't know which one of those opponents in the tug of war will answer you! And why is that? Well, just like anyone else, there have been times I've been bursting with pride at the real me and put a handful of colored sprinkles on top and gave my cupcake self to someone else for a big tasty bite. And guess what? That person or heck, let's be honest, it's been more than ONE person, bit in with vigor and then spit cupcake insides all over my face. Note to self: don't offer cupcake anymore.

This is what I haven't deleted yet. It's about as raw as I can get in this forum right now. I'm still arguing with myself and toying with stuffing those things back where they came from; stuff, stuff, stuff them away. But I've realized I'm exhausted. I'm so tired of holding the lid on all that crap with all my strength. Keep it closed. Keep it in. Would it be so terrible to bust open that Pandora's box? Would it be easier? Easier than trying so desperately to keep it squirreled away? So far it feels better. So far cracking that lid just a bit-while scary to look inside-is a such a relief, such a release of pressure. Lately I feel like I can't do it anymore. I can't hold the lid on. I'm just tired out. Good grief; if that's not vulnerable I don't know what is.

So there it is. It's not so bad. Go ahead and take a look inside. Just don't expect NOT to find a shit storm. We've all got one. But the truth is, I can't think of one time someone handed me their smelly pile of poo and I turned away. Never. Not once. The exchange always brought us to a place of being equal; being viewed as one in the same.

Today, a friend invited me to a yoga class. You know why I don't want to go? She just texted me that we will be barefoot. No socks? No sneakers? Okay I'm not going. My toes are so gross. My second toe is literally like a half inch longer than the first. I call them my gorilla feet. I can pick anything up with my feet. They're so nasty looking. So I'm out. Can't show those feet, no way. Vulnerability. Sticks to us like a freaking wad of gum on the bottom of our shoes.

Underneath it all I think is a fear of being alone. A fear that if you see me and turn away, I'll have to feel that stab of rejection again and again every time I think of you. So here's my hypothesis: If we can surround ourselves with enough supportive people who accept us, shit storm and all, than we can be alone with our discomfort and be okay with it. We can be by ourselves but know that we are connected to someone and never really alone. Connected. Whole. Accepted. Are those words the antonyms of vulnerable? I think they should be.

Perhaps it's easier to show our true selves with the support of someone else. I remember one time being home all day with two sick kids and the doorbell kept ringing. Now being in the news business as long as I have and growing up in New York, you ring my bell, if I'm not expecting you, I am NOT opening the door. No way. Especially not when I'm alone inside with two kids. But on this day, literally once an hour the doorbell would ring-of course just when I would get someone settled to sleep. So I glanced out my second-floor window to see who the heck this was. Didn't know the guy but I watched him and saw he was going door to door throughout my neighborhood. Hour by hour went by and I grew more and more angry. My husband came home around 9:00pm. I greeted him with a litany of complaints and outrage and instructed him to be my hero and chew this guy out if he rang the bell again. Not 15 minutes later-ding dong. My husband proceeds to the door and opens it ready to save his damsel in distress. Before the guy could even open his mouth for whatever solicitation he had intended, I literally pushed my husband out of the way and began my string of "You have some nerve.." and "You have been ringing my doorbell" and I'm sure some choice curse words came out of my mouth too. We closed the door and my husband turned to me and chuckled, "Well I'm glad I handled that!"

Clearly on that day, it was his love and support that made me brave. And wow did it feel good to let what I was really feeling out!

I think it is our vulnerability that makes us attractive to other people but it is also our vulnerability that stands in our way sometimes. I can think of dozens of scenarios when my efforts to hide an aspect of myself held me back-kept me from a full experience or from truly understanding a situation and it's outcome. Brene Brown, in her book, *The Gifts of Imperfection,* says, "Embracing our vulnerabilities is risky but not nearly as dangerous as giving up on love and belonging and joy; the experiences that make us the most vulnerable. Only when we are brave enough to explore the darkness will we discover the infinite power of our light." Problem is the "explore the darkness" part isn't so easy. Takes courage to plunge into something that might make us uncomfortable.

When she was in high school, one day my daughter said, "I've decided to let my freak flag fly." Now let me tell you, she is by no means any kind of freak, but what's more vulnerable than being in high school? This concept was her way of recognizing that she wasn't a carbon copy of everyone else and that would be stunning to some and thrilling to others, but she was going to hang it all out there. Enlightened that girl is!

So unpack your washing machine, set off your shit storm and I'll join you in a yoga class, gorilla feet and all.

Kim Howie:

Simply stated, vulnerability is having the courage to allow your true self to be seen! It takes courage to remove your mask and armor and let others see the real you. It can be scary to feel emotionally exposed, but opening yourself up and letting others in is vital for authentic connection.

You may have been conditioned to see vulnerability as weakness, but in fact, it takes a strong person to own their truth, to stand tall and be brave when they feel uncomfortable! Brene Brown, Ph.D., LMSW and author of *Daring Greatly*, says that vulnerability is the core of all emotions and feelings. She states that to feel is to be vulnerable. So if we believe that vulnerability is weakness, then we believe that having feelings of any kind makes us weak.

Dr. Brown states that vulnerability is the birthplace of love, belonging, joy, courage, empathy, and creativity. It is the source of hope, empathy, accountability, and authenticity. And she proclaims that if we want greater clarity in our purpose or deeper and more meaningful spiritual lives, vulnerability is the path.

I have always been good at being vulnerable, at least that's what I thought! To me, vulnerability means letting others see you for who you really are, warts and all. It means not putting on "the face" or a facade to protect yourself from others. I was never good at hiding my feelings, nor did I really want to. I've always enjoyed sharing my inner thoughts with others and hearing theirs in return. To me, that's what true connection is all about.

But recently I was cracked wide open inside by the fear of being vulnerable in front of a television audience. I wrote earlier in the book about my fear of recording The Wisdom Coalition television show, and this fear sent me on a journey to uncover the root cause. After pulling back the layers of the proverbial onion, I realized that my fear was rooted in vulnerability. Being seen "as is" and judged for not being _____ enough (you can fill in the blank with smart, good, worthy, pretty, thin, etc.) Our "living out loud" social media culture enables people to say and post whatever comes to their minds, which is oftentimes things they wouldn't say to your face. Being a sensitive person, just the thought of hearing/reading something negative about myself brought immediate fear and sadness to my mind. This was when I realized that I wasn't as comfortable with vulnerability as I had thought.

What I recognized is that there is a difference between being vulnerable with people you know and trust, those who you believe will take care of your heart, verses being vulnerable with others who may not have your best interest at heart. Brene Brown talks about this in her book *Daring Greatly*, using the analogy of an arena, taken from Theodore Roosevelt's speech "Citizenship in a Republic." During the speech, Roosevelt states that it is not the critic who counts, but rather the person who is in the arena striving to make a difference. Brown says "we must walk into the arena, whatever it may be - a relationship, an important meeting, our creative process, or a difficult family conversation - with courage and the willingness to engage. Rather than sitting on the sidelines and hurling judgment, we must dare to show up and let ourselves be seen. This is vulnerability."

We all experience vulnerability differently. For me, sometimes it feels like heaven; that safe space where you can just be yourself and not worry about what others think. Sometimes it feels like hell; that place where you feel the spotlight is shining on all of your imperfections and others are lurking in the shadows hurling judgment at you. While oftentimes it feels like a combination of both depending on the circumstances. In an ideal world, one filled with love and compassion for ourselves and others, vulnerability would be commonplace and we would all feel free to just be who we are at all times without fear or judgment.

Ultimately, the TV experience helped me to grow. It forced me to dig deep and find the strength to really analyze that fear, and recognize that I am more than my ego, which tends to worry about what others think of me. And back to what I'd tell my younger self, you can't please everyone all of the time. What matters most is that I'm living MY truth and being the best version of myself that I can possibly be! And when I feel myself slipping back into old habits, instead of beating myself up, I remind myself of our shared humanity and the fact that we are all doing the best we can in life, and that's all that we can ask for.

Thought-Provoking, Self-Reflection Questions:
1. When do you feel the most vulnerable?
2. Does fear of vulnerability hold you back in life?
3. Can you see that vulnerability is true courage?

_____

_____

_____

_____

_____

_____

_____

_____

_____

_____

_____

_____

_____

_____

_____

_____

_____

_____

_____

_____

_____

_____

_____

_____

Chapter 22 - Aging Gracefully

Carmen Toro
Owner of Beauty Alibi
Professional make-up artist
Mother of three boys

"Aging with grace for me at this point in my life even though I'm a make-up artist and it's all about skin care, make-up, anti-aging products and the way you look, it's the way you accept yourself inside and that will come out in every situation or conversation and in everyday living. It's the beauty you have inside that is projecting outside."

Nancy Werteen:

If fate allowed you one moment to relive, what would it be? Would you repeat something wonderful or turn back the clock to avoid something awful? If you somehow had a golden ticket that gave you the power for just one moment, what would that moment be? Not an easy decision.

I remember a couple of months after I had my second daughter. She had just started sleeping through the night and I felt human again. I came out of my sleep-deprived haze and began to see her differently. Her tiny fingers rested so delicately in mine. This moment I snuggled up next to her on my bed in the middle of the afternoon, just to enjoy her. She gazed at me and tried her best to make sounds. She raised her eyebrows and looked intently at each aspect of my face. She worked desperately to coordinate her hands and get them to land on my face but they kept missing. I picked up her hand and kissed her fingers. Bliss.

This would be my last child. I would never get this moment back. I tried to memorize everything about it. Her pink sleeper with the bunnies on it couldn't have been softer. She smelled lovely, a mix of baby wipes and diaper rash cream. My hand caressed her soft, nearly bald head.

What if I could feel that sweet, amazing sensation of a newborn in my arms? Would that be the moment I would choose?

My eyes still glaze over when I think of the day my older daughter made her first Communion. We handmade her veil together. I can still see it cascading over the lumpy bun I wrestled her hair into. I can hear her voice as she walked from the altar right to me. She sang with the other children, "I believe there are angels among us." I see her reaching out as she handed me a white carnation. Is that the moment?

Is it the moment she safely woke up from emergency surgery two years later? Is it the moment of her birth after 28 hours of struggle? Or would I pick a moment that had nothing to do with my children?

Is it the moment my husband kissed me for the first time as his wife? The time he got in the shower with all of his clothes on to comfort me in an especially difficult time? Or our first kiss when he dropped the grocery bags he held to put his arms completely around me?

Is it the moment I first shared a joke with my parents as an adult instead of a child? Or just sitting with them and enjoying a cup of tea?

Would I want to be 17 again and delve back into one of the long summer nights I spent with girlfriends at the beach laughing and swearing we'd always be friends?

Is it friendship, love, or would I decide to stop time and keep my car from colliding with that checkered cab? Decide to stay on my feet instead of falling off that curb?

There are so many moments to consider, to remember, to relish and to regret. To me, aging gracefully has to do with learning to cherish these moments. It has to do with understanding that you can't go back and you have to appreciate the delights you have when you have them. It's about focusing on what you know is special and putting it on the pedestal it deserves to be on. That's what you learn as you age. How fleeting life is. You learn to hold on to love and kindness as long as you can. These are the memories that keep you company, that share your bed.

I think aging gracefully also has to do with relaxing into it. We were doing a podcast recently on this subject and I remembered a time in a step aerobics class some 10 years ago. Had myself nestled in the back, not too close to that mirror. With three rows or so of 20-and 30-year-old ladies' bottoms in my full view, I had this awful realization. I could do these steps and squats from sun up to sun down and my ass will never look like that again. I mean never. I could get some butt lift I guess but everything around my butt is still going to scream my age.

I remember a time when I actually used to go out for the night at 10:00pm. Go out!!! You could put a million dollars down on a bet that any day you look in on me at 10:00pm, I'm in my jammies doing "touch and go's" with my head on the couch. Heck, I might even be in bed already with that sleep number set to zero G. But it's my time, isn't it? I had my time to stay out until 5:00 in the morning. But now, you'd literally have to give me $10,000 to make me choose to do that.

It's time to embrace my age, meaning I have to see my limitations but still reach for the joys, opportunities and accomplishments that I always have. That's graceful if you ask me. Understanding where we are and making the very, very most of it. Embracing every stage we're in with the knowledge that our lives are fluid and fleeting.

My life is a compilation of moments that matter and my age is just the vehicle to house them in, to pull them out and replay the films with grace and fondness for all that is, all that was, and all that can be.

Kim Howie:

When we are younger, we wish away our youth, longing for the days when we are older and can do "whatever we want." I know my children are doing that right now. And I'm constantly telling them to slow down and enjoy their youth. My youngest hates going to school. Every night without fail she says "I don't want to go to school tomorrow," to which I respond "going to school is FUN! You'll miss going to school when you grow up!" Yes, it seems like we are always wishing to grow up when we are young, and then looking back and longing for our youth when we grow older!

I remember sitting outside with a long-time friend one day many years ago as she talked about how much she hated the age spots on her hands. I looked down at my hands and said "you mean these things? Oh, I always thought they were sunspots, not age spots." That was the beginning of the shift in my mind, I started scanning my body for more signs of aging. Looking for gray hairs and wrinkles. I was in my mid 30s at the time and had never really given much thought to aging, especially not any negative thoughts. In my mind, we were still young!

It's funny how the older I get the younger older people seem! I remember when I used to think that 50 was old. Now I think 70 is still young!! I've come to believe that age is just a mindset. One of my favorite quotes on aging comes from Dr. Christiane Northrup, author of *Goddesses Never Age*. She says "growing older is mandatory, but aging is optional." It's so true. Time will pass and we will grow older, but aging is all about how we choose to perceive ourselves at any given age. There are centenarians who are still young at heart. And I believe the reason they've lived to be over 100 years old is because they never let their age impact their state of mind.

I tell my children that I'm going to live to be 120 years old. I say this to be funny, but in reality, it's certainly within possibility. Especially with the medical advances that are made every day. The key is to take care of your body, mind, and spirit, and never let your physical age dictate your wellbeing!

I like to think of growing older as a gift. One that many people are not fortunate enough to receive. There are so many lives that are cut short by accidents, mishaps or diseases. When I wake up each morning, I feel blessed to be alive. My alarm goes off to the song Happy by Pharrell Williams, and I start my day with the intention to be happy. I try to remind myself to live life to the fullest and never take anything or anyone for granted. I believe that each day is a new opportunity to enjoy life.

Thought-Provoking, Self-Reflection Questions:
1. How do you view your age?
2. How do you feel about getting older?
3. What does aging with grace mean to you?

_____

_____

_____

_____

_____

_____

_____

_____

_____

_____

_____

_____

_____

_____

_____

_____

_____

_____

_____

_____

_____

_____

_____

_____

_____

Chapter 23 - Finding Your Authentic Self

Lindsay Watson
VP of Client Relations
FIA NYC Employment services

"In a society where there's so much consumerism, it can be easy to get caught up in trying to look like, act like, or speak like somebody else. However, we're all unique individuals. I believe just like puzzle pieces, if we were to be okay with who we are as an individual then we can see how we can benefit one another and help each other to grow."

Nancy Werteen:

I never leave my house without makeup on. Even if I'm in a rush and only going to the grocery store, I think, "just a little mascara." Well if I put on mascara, I might as well add eyeliner. Now eyeliner and mascara just look weird without foundation or at least powder. And for Heaven's sake if I put on powder, I have to add blush and throw in a contouring powder for good measure. And there you have it-a full face of makeup to go run an errand! Growing up on Long Island in the late 70s, early 80s, no respectable female would be seen without all her aesthetic ducks in a row, which was the theme of those decades of big hair, bold colors and really cheesy outfits. I guess that's where I get it from.

I've noticed most younger women (my college-aged daughter included) aren't like this. They think nothing of being less than "put-together" when they head out the door. They pull their hair back in a ponytail, tug on sweats and a sport bra and call it an ensemble. I have to say, I envy them a little. I wish I could have that sort of free spirit but it just isn't in me. My presentation to the world is buttoned up. So now

I'm wondering why. Why don't I leave my glasses on, skip the make up and do what I have to do? Well one time I had laryngitis and pink eye in both eyes and I had to get something at the store, a prescription maybe. So I have no makeup on, no voice and I throw on a baseball cap. I buy whatever it is that I need and the cashier hands me my bag with a cheery, "Have a nice day SIR!" Okay, that's why I have to polish a little to take on the world. The lack of boobs, the height and the gangliness don't lend themselves well to the natural look.

But what else is underneath my apprehension? I'd say it's fear. I've struggled with not only finding my authentic self but with unleashing her to the world. Don't we all do this? We keep so many relationships on the surface because God forbid someone sees what's REALLY inside! We create an image we want to put out to the world and work hard to cultivate and sustain it. How else can we protect ourselves? If someone rejects the facade we put out, who cares? That's not really who we are anyway. We're safe. We're in our cocoon. Dark. Quiet. Safe. I think we retreat there because we've all felt the blow of rejection, ridicule and betrayal.

On the other side of that internal argument are the times we've carefully chosen someone to see who we really are and that person has applauded and cherished us from head to toe. I think the struggle becomes: which feeling do you want more of? Of course, we want more of the acceptance and the gratitude we feel for it. Maybe we can couch the rejection in a softer equation, something like: maybe we just weren't the right fit for that other person. Maybe it's not that there's anything wrong with us, it's just that the timing was off.

Seems to me the more we risk putting our true selves in front of other people, the more we increase our chances of having real, meaningful relationships that make life worth living. Now I'm not saying it's a good idea to show up at your next business meeting in your pajamas with a bowl of chocolate ice cream reciting Christmas carols because that makes you happy. I'm saying check in with yourself. Evaluate who you are revealing your true self to and who you aren't and question yourself about it.

This is what I've been doing in this process of writing this book and I have to say about three-quarters of the way through it, I teetered on the corner of a nervous breakdown of sorts. I guess it's the mid-life thing. Suddenly, I felt I might just have my mid-life crisis. What is that anyway? The dictionary says a mid-life crisis is: an emotional crisis of identity and self-confidence that can occur in early middle age. Yeah, that's what it was. Thinking about all these subjects and squeezing the mental toothpaste out of my brain took some courage at first, some strength second and then some anti-nausea medication third. I haven't been completely thrilled with everything I've seen inside once I began looking. And as much as I closed my eyes when it got too scary, I have forced myself to open them again. I'm realizing that looking in the rearview mirror is great, you just can't keep looking there. Glance back, sure. But look ahead or you're seriously going to slam into something.

Before this, the term "finding your authentic self" confused me. Who the heck else am I going to find? Where would I be? But then I connected the dots and realized there can be a disconnect between who you are, who you think you are and who the world sees. My goal is to try to align all those three things but I recognize my work isn't finished here, it's just getting started.

A few years ago, when my husband and I celebrated our 20th wedding anniversary, I told him, "This is as good as it's going to get." Meaning me-not the relationship. And I followed that up with, "And I'm going to let you see everything because I'm frankly too old to have the energy to polish it up anymore." Something like that anyway. I had rehearsed my little speech for days thinking I was making some grand life changing declaration that he might reject me for. I had no reason to think this except for the fear I had activated in myself. He listened and quickly said, "Fantastic! I want it all." Whew. I walked on the limb and he was there to catch me. Doesn't get much better than that.

Kim Howie:

When we talk about finding our authentic self, it seems like it should be easy, right? Who could possibly know us better than we know ourselves? But we tend to put on different masks for the many different roles we play in our lives; one for work, one for home, one for close friends, one for social acquaintances and so on. Some of our masks serve as armor to protect us from the outside world, while others were created to help us fit in. With all of these different masks, it gets confusing to figure out who we really are.

So how do we uncover our authentic self? Our authentic self is who we are at our core; the person behind the mask. Uncovering that person is a process similar to peeling back the layers of an onion.

Building awareness is the first step. We all know that feeling of pretending to be something we are not, whether it's to fit in or it's to cover up pain, it's simply not being our authentic self. Building awareness is simply taking notice when we recognize that feeling and labeling it as such. It's also important to pay attention to who/what triggers us to armor up.

The next step involves soul searching and taking a good hard look inside ourselves. Once we realize that we are not feeling authentic, we must start to dig deeper to figure out why. Throughout life, we build barriers to protect ourselves in response to negative experiences we encounter on our journey. And oftentimes we fall into habitual response patterns, and our barriers go up without even thinking about it. The way to return to our true self is to identify and break down those barriers. Chip away at the armor we have worn to protect our hearts and let our inner light shine for all to see. Challenge any dominant stories that are keeping us stuck behind our masks. And recognize that it takes vulnerability to be brave enough to share our true self with the world.

The final step involves remaining true to your authentic self. Our authentic self is a culmination of our deepest values and our inner truth. So in order to find our authentic self, we need to identify our values and ensure that our actions are in alignment with them. This is an ongoing process that takes time and attention.

There are many tools available to help us identify our values, but one that I love is a free online assessment called the VIA (Values in Action). You can take the assessment at www.viacharacter.org. Personally, I found this tool to be extremely helpful. I'd love to hear your experience! Email me at thewisdomcoalition@gmail.com if you'd like to share.

I believe that we are all here on a journey together, and part of that journey includes the process of finding our authentic selves and learning to love them and each other unconditionally.

Thought-Provoking, Self-Reflection Questions:
1. Do you know your authentic self?
2. Have you ever felt that you were putting on a mask?
3. What are your core values and are your actions in alignment with them?

_____

_____

_____

_____

_____

_____

_____

_____

_____

_____

_____

_____

_____

_____

_____

_____

_____

_____

_____

_____

_____

_____

Chapter 24 - Joy:
The Top 10 Ways To Connect To Your Inner Joy

Lisa Fichera
Executive VP and COO of Phoebe Ministries
Caregiver to her late father for 5 years

"I believe human kindness will prevail . We have a lot of challenges in the world but I think the positives are always going to push forward. "

Nancy Werteen:

So there you have it. 23 Chapters and a lot to think about. If you made it this far, hopefully you've discovered some wonderful things about yourself or maybe you've turned some corners, changed some aspects of your outlook, made some decisions. Or maybe you've just listened and contemplated. We like to think you've joined us for a cup of tea and some good conversations about what we call "the mushroom topics." These are challenging feelings that grow when you keep them in the dark. Our hope is that this book project is a beacon of light for you-that you are working to strengthen what you like about your outlook and figuring out how to release what isn't working for you anymore. That's a term Kim uses a lot. She always says, "Think about how that is or isn't serving you." For me, I've found many things in these pages that I realize haven't been serving me very well at all. Without them, I have room for the things that do. And that's the whole point. Once you make the space, there's room for better things like joy and hope and serenity. That's what we want you to have-space to fill with the wonderful things that delight you.

Now, we've come full circle. We've come to the realization that is the foundation of our message to you. Joy, my dear friends, is totally up to you. It's your choice. We thank you for taking this ride with us. We hope you've loved it as much as we have. We will leave you with the most important message we have-that you control your future. You drive the bus. Take it where you want to go. Here's how:

First we must recognize that there is "Inner Joy" in all of us; it is an innate gift we all have. Once we are aware of this gift, we will become empowered to take control of the amount of joy we experience in our lives every day. However, to achieve more joy, we need to be open to change. We have to understand that we may have to make a few changes in our lives or daily routines. We have to allow ourselves to be open to new possibilities for ourselves and our future. Below are our top 10 suggestions for increasing your inner joy. We can think of each step as though we are planting a seed for Joy to blossom within us. We must trust that this seed of Joy will blossom if we continue to nurture it.

1. Choose joy

We need to consciously CHOOSE joy! It is a choice we all can make - even in our most trying moments, joy is there. We've all heard the adage that happiness is a choice. Yet, sometimes we forget that WE control our thoughts, not the other way around, even though we often allow our thoughts to control us. Choosing joy requires us to live mindfully in the present moment, building awareness around how we react to people and circumstances that are outside of our control. By simply reminding ourselves that we can choose joy at any time, we take back our personal power allowing us to be happy regardless of the circumstances. In this way we are experiencing unconditional joy.

2. Create a routine to cultivate joy

The next step is to rethink our daily routines and participate in more activities that fill us with joy and less that deplete us of our joy. We may need to let go of old habits and develop new ones that will guide us to a healthier and happier lifestyle. Living a life filled with joy takes practice. It's like building a muscle over time that will eventually become self-sustainable. When we start and end our day with a gratitude ritual (such as writing in a journal or giving thanks), it becomes a habit similar to brushing our teeth, where we won't feel right if we don't do it. It's important to realize that there is joy all around us, even if that joy is simply the awareness of the stars in the sky or the comfort of our bed each night. Many of us put off our joy waiting to reach a milestone (I'll be happy when….I get a promotion at work, I meet my soulmate, I move into my dream house, etc.), but we need to be thankful for where we are on our way to where we want to be.

3. Shift your perspective

But it is not always that easy, and it takes practice! We need to learn to reframe our thoughts when we notice negativity consuming our minds. The more we practice this reframing, in different situations, we will become more likely to think positively and optimistically. Soon it may become a natural instinct to automatically choose thoughts of joy above all else. This concept is referred to as learned optimism.

It's important to recognize that our perspective in life is what forms our own personal reality. Have you ever noticed how two people can experience the same situation in life and come away with completely different impressions of what happened? This is primarily because we run our experiences through our own filters and see life through different lenses. We see things in life not as they are, but as we are. Dr. Wayne

Dyer, author and philosopher, spoke these true words: "change the way you look at things and the things you look at change." Therefore, if we shift our perspective and focus on positive aspects of life, our perceptions of life will in turn be more positive.

4. Reframe your thoughts and learn to think like an optimist!

When we are feeling disconnected from joy, we need to recognize that by simply changing our thoughts to view things more positively, we can change how we feel. We have the ability to choose to see life as an opportunity for growth and expansion. This may require some practice and awareness of our tendency to see life as difficult and full of struggles. However, once we become aware of our negative thoughts, we can work to reframe them into more positive language. Rather than saying "I HAVE TO (go to work, take my children to their activities, do the laundry, etc.)," we can say "I GET TO (go to work, take my children to their activities, do the laundry, etc.)." This small change in language reframes our thoughts to be grateful for the ability to GET to do these things in life.

5. Look for the lesson in all experiences

When things don't work out in our favor, we must trust that there is a lesson to be learned. Most people are searching for the meaning of life. Why are we here? If life is intended to be fulfilling, then we should be open to evolving and learning along the way. Therefore, if we alter our view to recognize that life is happening FOR us rather than TO us, we will see all experiences as an opportunity to learn and grow. This enables us to seek and find the silver lining in adverse life experiences and be grateful for the hidden lesson.

6. Create your own reality

What we look for in life is what we see. Have you ever noticed that if you go into a situation thinking that it will be negative, it almost always is? This is because you are unconsciously looking for things to confirm your belief that it will be a bad experience. Yet the good news is that the same rules apply for the positive. If we decide that we are going to have a good experience before we begin, we typically look for things to validate THAT belief. Therefore, if we make our minds up to be happy each day, we will create a much more joyful reality as we watch the world around us change.

7. Set your own personal standards and stop comparing yourself to others

We are all unique and have something special to share with the world. Many times in life we stand in our own light, creating the shadow we feel within. We need to stop comparing ourselves to others and set our own personal standards based on our individual strengths. Comparison truly is the thief of joy. If we need to compare, we should only compare ourselves to our former selves to ensure that we are growing and evolving.

We tend to be our own worst critics in life. We talk to ourselves in ways that we would never dream of speaking to someone else. We tell ourselves that we are not good enough, not smart enough, not pretty enough, simply not enough. We tend to set low expectations for our joy because we don't believe that we are worthy of more. The truth is that we are all worthy and are inherently enough!

If we simply stop comparing, get out of our own way and let go of self-limiting beliefs, we can set and reach higher expectation and recognize that we are worthy of living a joy-filled life.

8. Honor your body and your spirit will soar

We must also remember to love ourselves first because lasting joy radiates from within. It starts from the inside, and your health matters A LOT when it comes to continuously cultivating joy. It's important to recognize that what we eat affects how we feel, both physically and emotionally. The old adage of "you are what you eat" is more accurately stated as "you feel like what you eat." When you eat crap, you feel crappy.

When we choose nourishing foods, our body responds by providing us with increased energy and clearer thinking. Honoring our bodies with healthy foods and proper self-care increases our overall well-being and enables our spirits to soar.

9. Live your life from the inside out

Oftentimes we allow the outside world to dictate our degree of happiness. We look to our spouse, our children, our friends, etc. to bring us joy. However, that is backwards. We need to fuel our core energy with joy and allow that energy to drive our thoughts, actions and feelings. We must recognize that our thoughts, actions and feelings are all interrelated such that each influences the other. And remember that WE control our thoughts and actions, and therefore our feelings! When we increase the quality of our thoughts, we instantly elevate our feelings and are open to experience more joy and unlimited bliss.

10. Stay connected to your WHY

It's so important that we know and understand the driving force behind every choice we make in life. When we remember why we chose to start something (whether it's a career choice, a relationship, or a lifestyle choice), staying connected to our why enables us to stay on track and stay motivated.

Our personal why doesn't need to make sense to anyone except us. There's no need to defend your why or explain it to anyone else. What matters most is that you stay connected to it and allow it to drive you forward and fill you with joy!

These are the principles upon which The Wisdom Coalition was created. We believe that positive thoughts lead to positive results, and don't we all want that in our lives?! A positive, optimistic perspective will encourage us to nurture and care for ourselves. As a result, we learn that there is an abundance of JOY available to all of us. Once we learn to honor ourselves, our joy becomes contagious and naturally attracts others who seek the same things as us. We want to surround ourselves with others who know the power of joy and how it fosters limitless personal growth.

Lastly, although this is all about connecting to YOUR inner joy, we must not forget that human connection is the best way to bring out the joy within. But this human connection must be genuine and authentic. We must learn to live as our authentic selves to experience the true power of joy.

ACKNOWLEDGMENTS

We would like to thank you, our readers, for having the courage to examine yourselves.

Thank you to our families, our husbands and our children, who have been patient and supportive of the time we've spent on the computer, on the phone, texting and talking about our ideas and hopes for this book and The Wisdom Coalition.

Thank you to Gignere Publishing for believing in us. Thank you to Dr. Nichola Gutgold, who invited us into the backyard garden of her home on a sunny afternoon to share our vision. We are so grateful for your endless support, your spectacular ideas and for sharing your wisdom of the publishing world with us! Thank you also for your endless energy, praise and encouragement to continue "onward!"

Thank you to all of the wonderful supporters of The Wisdom Coalition for recognizing our purpose has value and for your kind comments and advice. Special thanks to our Wisdom Advisors who have helped to chart our course. A shout-out to all the women along the way who listened to our vision and said, "What a great idea!"

Praise to WFMZ-TV69 in Allentown, PA for having so much faith in our concept to give us our own television show. Thank you to all of our guests on our television program and podcasts.

Special thanks to freelance copywriter Maria Costa Woytek for her careful eye, incredible knowledge and loving support.

Thank you to Terree Yeagle, owner of The Moment Photography and Wear The Wonder for sharing her vast artist talents that created the photographs for our book.

Thank you to the subscribers of The Wisdom Coalition newsletter for the encouraging feedback and for asking for more.

And finally, we'd like to thank each other for allowing ourselves the freedom to argue our creative side of each project; for always making sure to make time for our friendship and the deep meaning that it has for us; for giving ourselves the license and acceptance to laugh out loud and make jokes when frustrations slipped into the process; and for teaching each other the true meaning of unconditional love.

To find out more about the Wisdom Coalition, our Well of Wisdom, our events, podcasts, programs, television show and how to become a subscriber, go to www.thewisdomcoalition.com.

Go to our website to purchase our Wisdom Symbol pendant (seen below) so you can always have a reminder close to your heart to live your life from the inside out!

Sources Cited:

Brene Brown, *Daring Greatly*, Avery Publishing, 2015.

Brene Brown, *The Gifts of Imperfection*, Hazelden Publishing, 2010.

Gary Chapman, *The Five Languages of Love*, Moody Publishers, 2010.

Elizabeth Gilbert, *Eat Pray Love*, Riverhead Books, 2007.

Susan Jeffers, *Fear the Fear and Do It Anyway*, Ballantine Books; 20th Anniversary edition, 2006.

Marie Kondo, *The Life Changing Magic of Tidying Up*, Penguin House, 2015.

Christina Northrup, *Goddesses Never Age*, Avery Publishing; Reprint edition, 2015.

Cheryl Richardson, *The Art of Extreme Self Care*, Hay House Publishing, 2009.

Other Words of Wisdom Provided By:

Maya Angelou

Dr. Wayne Dyer